Leadership

Elevate Yourself and Those around You

Influence, Business Skills, Coaching &

Communication

Image: Public Domain Pixabay

Ross Elkins

Ross Elkins

Disclaimer Notice:

Please note the information contained within this document is for educational and entertainment purposes only. Every attempt has been made to provide accurate, up to date and reliable complete information. No warranties of any kind are expressed or implied. Readers acknowledge that the author is not engaging in the rendering of legal, financial, medical or professional advice.

Table of Contents

Ross Elkins

Introduction

Before we start, I would like to make few statements about differences between a leader and a manager. A leader makes decisions and sets up goals, then he or she will lead his or her team members toward those goals. A leader has a group of followers. With collaboration, communication and trust, they stand united and face every challenge together to achieve their desired goals in the short and long term. On the other hand, a manager is someone who wants their employees to work for them. Managers have subordinates or employees but that does not necessarily make them leaders. Managers have a position of authority vested in them by the company, and their employees work for them and largely do as they are told. They thus naturally pass on this work focus to their employees.

What makes a successful leader like Steve Jobs, Mark Zuckerberg and other entrepreneurs of this magnitude? There is a long-standing debate about whether leaders are born or made to become successful leaders. Some people possess the inherent qualities of a good leader, while others have to cultivate such qualities. Did they have a formal education or have they experienced the real business world or were they influenced by physical and emotional environmental influences? However, there is no rule that declares natural leaders better than those who have honed their skills to match those required of a leader. In the corporate world, leadership is one of the most sought-after qualities in an employee. This natural aptitude or learned skill helps them to lead others into success. A successful team leads to a successful company or business. If you are in a managerial position, you are expected to handle a team, nurture them, motivate them, inspire them, constantly communicate with them and ensure the best possible outcome and productivity from the team to achieve your team's objectives. All of this cannot be achieved without possessing the skills of a strong leader. Your team is like a boat and you are the captain. You have to lead your sailors and engineers to a destination by going through storms, big waves and even taking on "pirates." You need to understand the course and choose a right path that will subsequently bring you to designated destination.

Leadership can be defined as the process of influencing the behavior of one's subordinates, without making them feel like they are working under a dictatorship. A leader will use his/her authority, but as a coach who guides and leads the team to achieve set goals. It is the social process of directing people in the way that you see fit, helping them visualize a common goal and invoking the drive to achieve it. Leadership is not about achieving objectives or goals without taking care of your team. It is all about bringing your whole team together onto the battlefield, and harnessing their abilities into a joint effort to achieve a significant vision. This could be hard if you lack leadership skills such as communication skills and motivational skills. Whenever your team is facing a problem, you have to stand out from the crowd and give the team motivation to move forward. You have to put your "Managerial authority" down and show all the traits of a leader.

A good leader is able to identify past, existing and upcoming problems and then prescribe a strategic plan to deal with those problems. Successful leaders such as Apple founder, Steve Jobs and Google founder, Larry Page are great examples good leaders who have overcome their problems with brilliant and unique solutions. Every time you hear about the release a new product, it is totally new to the industry and leaders such as these keep on improving what is offered in a fast changing world. Leaders are expected to push the boundaries of their corporate setting, see the bigger picture and emerge with a mission that team members are going to be able to work toward in achieving the prescribed objective. Leaders are different from managers in that while managers focus on supervising their subordinates and managing problems by themselves instead of working with those employees as a team, leaders focus on motivation and lead their subordinates into overcoming problems and seeking out strategic actions to be taken to enable change.

Leaders are not built overnight. If you want to act as an effective leader, especially in today's fast changing world, you must allow yourself to constantly evolve quickly enough to adapt to the existing environment. For example, if you are not familiar with using technology software such as Paypal, Salesforce and so on and it's relevant to your work, you have to learn it first, in order to ease your task. Always read news and gain knowledge to stay ahead of anyone else because that's what leaders do. You must allow for constant change in global trends and workforce diversity factors and use this knowledge in the way you deal with people. You need to be open minded to accept cross-cultural differences especially when working in a diversified company. Leadership is about making effective decisions without causing conflict among employees. A good leader is someone who has confidence in his or her decisions. They are also creative and honest. They are able to delegate tasks to the right person, able to communicate with team members effectively and to show commitment within the team they are leading.

In this book, we will discuss about the finer nuances of what makes a good leader, and include strategies for leading in business, detailing expectations and demands and everything that comes into the leadership spectrum.

Ross Elkins

Chapter 1

Qualities of an Effective Leader

All successful leaders were once average children who did the same things that we did. Some people are born with an innate sense of leadership, and are good at making effective managerial decisions and leading their co-workers to maximum productivity, while others need a nudge in the right direction to realize their full potential when it comes to leadership. For this to happen, extroverts are naturally good in leadership as they are more open and communicate with everyone really easily. You would have noticed these kids in the school environment as they may have been leaders from their youth and may have these leadership qualities built into their characters.

One day, if you occupy a managerial position in a small or a medium company or a big corporate, you will find that it is expected of you to take effective decisions and lead people in order to fulfill the visions and goals of the company. For a good leader, it is significant to know how to lead, to influence and to communicate effectively. These skills are the prerequisites for anybody in a managerial leadership position where they are responsible for the growth of a company. However, many managers and leaders fail to figure this out and have difficulty practicing these requirements.

There are many arguable qualities that are essential for being a good leader. Some are inborn while some need to be developed and nurtured. The characteristics of a good leader involve these following personality traits:

Confidence and Self-assurance

Since leaders are responsible for the outcome of the group, it is prudent for them to be absolutely sure about the decisions they will make. A confident approach and a strong belief in your own abilities are inspiring traits. Based on surveys done by researchers, group members are more likely to follow someone who is willing to tackle a problem head-on with confidence and unwavering spirit. Leaders who are sure that they are making the right decisions, and do not seek approval or have doubts show resilience. They believe what they have decided and are willing to take the risk without consulting their team members for opinions because a leader should have a clearer and broader view than anyone else. Confident leaders command respect and inspire people to follow them to achieve the targeted objective and goals. With strong self-awareness, they know their strengths and weaknesses well and rarely surpass them.

They know when to ask for help from other team members and the risks they take on the job are well studied and analyzed. They won't ask for a challenge that they know they can't handle alone. They will overcome the risk with the whole team. One of the best ways to improve your confidence is to become aware of all of the things you've already achieved. Look back and recall the lessons you have learned and let this thought give you more inspiration and motivation.

To make a proper distinction, the respect that leaders command comes from providing a good example, and not solely by giving orders. You have to delegate the task to the right person who has the appropriate skills and lead that person with trust and belief in him or her. However, you have to clearly understand what your team and you can do and cannot do together. Evaluate the necessary skills and knowledge, and then delegate the task to right person. Never ask a fish to climb a tree. You are going to spend your whole life achieving nothing if you cannot work out appropriate roles for team members. If you have a financial task, you do not ask someone who is in the marketing department to do it. It sounds simple and common sense, but often many managers are bad at delegating tasks and cause their team to have weaknesses. Some employees work all day long but some walk around and communicate, encouraging staff to achieve. This is where inspiration develops in others. When they see someone exemplify the task or skill at hand, they are more inclined to attempt it themselves, and then they become willing to follow and contribute to that person's future endeavors and the larger scheme of things. Nobody likes to be controlled in his or her job and this can kill creativity that is hidden inside team members. Companies with open culture like Google, Facebook and Apple did a great job in maintaining a work/life balance in that meant that they had sufficient energy to give their best.

All other skills outlined in this book are rendered moot for the aspiring leader until they have cultivated or unless they naturally possess the confidence necessary to take on the role of leader. Everything provided in this book is merely statement if you do not want to change and take action. And confidence does not have to be this mystical seed for growing prosperity and influence either. If you think back to when you were a child and just went ahead and did things without contemplating all the "what if's," you will find that most of us have always possessed this quality and while some have forgotten they had it, others have just had more practice at exercising it over the years. When you grow older, your curiosity becomes weaker and you become less motivated to take risks. A true and successful leader is the man who likes to challenge their company with risk. They make risky decisions but with a good plan in mind, the risk being managed to follow on to success. They are confident about their abilities and their teamwork.

To cultivate confidence where it may appear to be lacking, a person has to tend the thoughts in their mind like a garden. In a garden, there are so many grasses that grow naturally. Some may be dangerous to your plants but they may bring benefits as well. They may increase food chain competition but they also help you to reduce competition in some other ways. You must identify any and every thought that exhibits self-doubt without trying to reason or justify why it's there and simply uproot it. Get rid of it, because there is absolutely no service a self-doubting thought can provide, other than a false sense of safety that actually prevents you from being at your best. A person must then tend to the positive thoughts they have about themselves and nurture them so that they grow along with their already noticeable traits. One must also plant seeds of positive thoughts in their fertile mind of how they see themselves at their best and even qualities they feel they don't currently exhibit but aspire to have. Without positive thoughts, you will feel demotivated and lose confidence in your work. You start to think about failure first and then start to doubt your abilities. For habitual self-doubters this may require a "fake it till you made it" approach. However, this process involves directly changing one's mindset, which will require ample amounts of practice and repetition no matter who the person is.

With time, enforcing those positive thoughts will begin give way to revealing themselves in personal behavior, and every external challenge that contends with those thoughts is a chance to exert one's confidence with both assertion and humility. Humility does not mean in the sense that one is weak, but quite the opposite; they are humble because they are sure of themselves without having to prove it.

Like the simple phrase, "monkey see, monkey do" *be* the example, set the standard and others will be compelled to recognize it and live up to it. Just like being a parent, our children tend to follow what we do and what we say to them. When you are confident and motivated, your employees will also feel the same way. They understand you are doing the best for them.

To be more confident in your job, you should have strong self-awareness. Self-awareness means having a deep understanding of ones emotions, strengths, weaknesses, needs and drives. Understanding yourself well can helps you to overcome the challenges and negative feedback by turning them into valuable sources to improve your weaknesses. Identify your strengths and capitalize on them, identify weaknesses, and work on them. With self-awareness, you can figure out your strengths and weaknesses, so when you are dealing with problems, you know yourself what your capabilities are. You know when to delegate your tasks to someone who has potential and to lead them.

Another way is to challenge yourself. Accomplishing things that you might think impossible to achieve can be a great way to boost your confidence. Find tasks, projects and assignments that give you an opportunity to use your strengths and take on projects that stretch you. This can include personal challenges by performing something that makes your heart beat stop a second each day. For example, walk up to someone on the street and tell him or her they are beautiful human being. Step out of your cozy comfort level.

Good communication skills

Communication within a team is crucial to stay on track, to identify and solve arising problems until achieving your targeted goals. How you perform as a good leader is heavily dependent on your ability to communicate with the team. Poor leaders don't value communication with their employees. A poor leader will spend long periods of time away from his desk or office or ignore staff emails and telephone messages. They tend to set a barrier to communication. A good leader is able to outline project objectives, state existing problems and chart strategies, delegating tasks in a very precise manner that leaves no room for error or confusion. You must be willing to share your valuable knowledge as that can contribute in the outcome. Knowledge is crucial for information sharing within the team. Poor communicators may also fail to pass along new information about company policies or procedures that will affect the way staff members perform their jobs. At the end of the day, the group leader is held accountable for the merits or demerits of the team, so the leader is expected to make sure that there is no lapse in understanding what a particular project entails. This is why good leader has to be confidence.

This is also why communication skills are crucial and perhaps under-appreciated in the cache of leadership resources. Of course, it would be ideal to present a project plan to a team then immediately set it into motion. However, a leader must deal with different perspectives and interpretations from team members. So while precise presentation is foremost in communication, there are a few other tactics to solidify a team's understanding as a unit. Besides, a good leader should have an "Open Door" policy. This is to encourage feedback, reduce office politics and help employees to realize that their opinions and thoughts do matter and have an impact on the team.

It is important for you to ensure your team or employees are doing the right things, but not just doing things right.

Good communicators are good listeners, often paraphrasing what the speaker said and checking in to ensure that they did not misinterpret the message. A good leader spends more time listening than talking. They show respect and listen carefully to the person who is talking. They let their speaker feel they are engaged in the communication and their problem about certain topics is taken into their consideration.

Today, there are so many distractions around us; it can significantly impact the quality of our listening skills and interpretation of the words we hear. For example, emails we send and receive through our smartphone applications are a typical example. Empathetic leaders put away their mobile phones, close their e-mail inboxes, and stay focused when listening, so all of their attention is on the speaker in front of them! They would rather spend their time listening to feedback than spending time surfing social networks. They always answer your questions and provide detailed feedback for you to help you to improve.

Ending a briefing or task delegation with concept-checking questions is one of the effective ways to ensure that each team member understands what is expected of him or her, and to pinpoint any areas that are not understood so that they may be clarified. You should always follow up either daily or weekly for their progress and problems. If they are facing any problems, you should guide them and give feedback for immediate improvement. When, your employees or team members receive your feedback, they will become more motivated and more productive in doing their work.

Alternatively, you can use internal communication tools such as email to keep in touch with him or her. Companies with highly effective internal communication networks such as IBM, Facebook and Google are using internal communication tools to communicate with their employees on an ongoing basis. However, it is strongly recommended communicating face to face when you can because you can observe their body language and increase your engagement with them. Also, you can easily get wrong interpretations on the words used in emails and messages. The way you write and writing formats such as capital letters have different meanings and are open to the wrong interpretation as some people see these letters as anger while others may see them as being comical. Therefore, misinterpretation can actually affect the morale of the team members.

Neuro Linguistic Programming, or NLP, is a study that is becoming more and more popular among leaders in business, education and other organizations. 'Neuro' refers to the applications and stimulation of the mind, 'Linguistic' speaks to the language we use, whether it is verbal or nonverbal, and 'Programming' suggests the patterns of thinking and behavior that we become accustomed to operating under.

We will cover more in detail about NLP in Chapter 3. For now, let us simply go over what it may provide for us in a leadership position. By employing NLP, not only when engaging others but in training our minds to think differently as well, we may better develop our communication skills, set convincing and approachable goals for ourselves and others, attain and nurture an increased self-awareness and awareness of others, gain an increased ability to influence and motivate others and better manage both personal and team performance.

NLP is often used to analysis personality traits for yourself and your employees. It can help you to categorize people into different groups. Each group has their own unique personalities such as risk takers, achievers, organizers and observers and more. It helps you delegate the task to right person to help maximize the outcome.

NLP is used more often in leadership coaching and pertains directly to understanding Emotional Intelligence so that the work environment may run more smoothly, as workers will become more apt to feel supported. Without it, a person can have the demanded leadership skills, but he still won't make a good leader.

Emotional Stability

A good leader is someone who does not let emotions cloud their judgment. Our emotions can easily be influenced by stresses arising from project problems, or our personal problems such as family and relationship problems. A good leader should have high level of Emotion Intelligence (EI). They are able to step back from their own personal feelings and understand the other person's feelings and analyze those feelings in a subjective manner. An effective and a good leader must, at all times, be ready to take on stress and turmoil, without giving into it and letting frustration affect their decision-making prowess. A good leader should not be biased against anyone in his or her team. This sounds easy enough until the stress actually hits you. There are many subtle ways that emotions can impact the decision-making process, so it becomes a leader's responsibility to manage a certain level of awareness within himself.

Emotional suppression is a common side effect of placing business and business-related tasks first, although it ultimately resurfaces in many different formats. Some of these formats may manifest as physical health issues such as high blood pressure, headaches or chronic muscle tension. Some are caused by mental health issues like depression, stress and anxiety. They may include subtle behavioral changes like aloofness, short temper or disconnection from employees or oneself, which may result in losing focus on the higher objectives. Many leaders feel regret whenever they achieve their goals in life at the expense of good health. As a really successful leader, you should know how to balance your work and your life. You need to live like a normal person after leaving your office.

Therefore, emotional stability in the high-stress business environment becomes a kind of dance where a leader must learn to exercise executive judgment in allowing themselves to feel their emotions without being carried away by them. Without bottling them up, a leader may develop emotional strength to their advantage, using it as fuel for directives and problem solving. For example, when a person becomes frustrated, without letting it cloud their judgment, they may use that feeling as a drive to do something about the situation at hand rather than just sitting on it. Consider the famous quote, "Within every problem lies opportunity." Putting it simply, you have to develop positive thinking in order to see opportunities. Negative thinking always makes you feel bad and fail to achieve certain goals.

In a managerial position, when you are responsible for the outcome of a group, for taking well-meaning decisions, you cannot let negative thoughts, anxiety, frustration, fatigue or other such emotional factors get to you. You must be well prepared to tackle high levels of stress and be emotionally equipped to ensure the same for those working with you.

To overcome these issues, you can express your feelings and thoughts to someone who is willing to listen. You can also exercise every day especially in the morning and that can also boost you productivity and improve your mental health in long term. Besides, if you are spiritual, you can perform meditation. There are many more ways you can improve your mental state such as keeping your mind active in some positive way.

Researchers have found that emotional intelligence is linked to strong performance in a company. The findings of the late David McClelland, the renowned researcher in human and organizational behavior, are a good example. In one of his studies, McClelland found that when senior managers had a critical mass of emotional intelligence capability, their divisions outperformed yearly earnings goals by 20%. Meanwhile, the managers who were short tempered or lacked emotional intelligence were more likely fail to reach their targeted sells.

Here are few useful tips and most importantly, they work!

- Accept the bad days – It is okay to have bad luck and to experience failures in your life. No one in the world achieves success without countless failures. Even Bill Gates and Warren Buffer said they often make mistakes. But, they never blame themselves for it. Instead, they take it as a good lesson to improve and learn from it by not to repeating it any more in future. The first mistake is a mistake; second mistake is choice.

- Get to know yourself more – Observe your emotion, attitude and behavior or ask for feedback from someone who is close or trustworthy. Controlling your emotions isn't about pretending they are not there. You have to face them in order to grow stronger mentally. Ask yourself what makes you feel bad, why you feel bad and how to improve your mood swings.

- Exercise - Exercise to relieve stress and lift your mood. Exercise is a powerful antidote to stress, anxiety and depression. Jogging in a park or garden is one of the best ways. Through it, you can communicate with someone while enjoying the natural environment. Another way is go to a gym to challenge your mental level and physical level, which are interconnected.

- Get enough rest. To have good mental and emotional health, it's important to take care of your body. That includes getting enough sleep. Most people need seven to eight hours of sleep each night in order to function optimally.

Boldness

A common trait among good leaders is their social aggressiveness and risk-taking nature. You see, they always be bold and take risky decision. In fact, they make decisions after they have studied the possible positive and negative consequences that will directly or indirectly affect their goals. They know how to achieve them, who they need and why they need to achieve these goals. While making corporate decisions, sometimes it is required that you take the plunge and go for a risky option that may potentially pay off really well. This is how many leaders stand out from the crowd and bring huge success to their companies. In such situations, a good leader weighs their options and does not shy away from taking a risk. After he or she has made the decision, he or she has to stay "FOCUSED", focusing on one course until this reaches success. Giving up is never their choice. They always find a solution together with their team, and do not do this alone.

I bet you never heard of Richard Branson if you are not paying attention to up and coming businesses. Branson is the founder of the company Virgin and one of the most successful leaders, personifying this quality by enterprising upon virtually every business sector in which he gets involved. Virgin's name is used because he is completely a "Virgin" or inexperienced in the business that he had started with his team. They took the risk that nobody wanted to take, and it paid off in a rewarding way. Since then, Branson's company has invested its efforts in music, cellphones, airlines, railways and even space shuttles. He is one who will not shy away from a risky venture and has seen his audacity pay off over and over again. Branson is one to advocate for following your gut when appropriate. When you feel strongly about it, sometimes you just have to go for it and take the risk. Sometimes that means investing yourself in a big way, but the rewards can be even bigger.

Some of the successful leaders also prompt us to believe in our instincts. Sometimes, we fear failure more than our desire to succeed. We fear being laughed at by someone, fear the loss in profit and so on. Successful leaders know how to manage and differentiate their fear and their desire to succeed well. This is why good leaders don't let fear control them, their actions, or those of their employees. Fear breeds anxiety among a number of other production-depreciative emotions that hinder progress and pinch off the lifeblood of a company. It is better to face fearful realities courageously than bury your head in the sands of bland work. Courage can be found in the workplace on multiple levels; it doesn't just have to be shown when investing in risky adventures.

Leaders often show boldness when they need to have conversations with employees, superiors and competitors that require an unattractive truth to be revealed and discussed. They are also bold when having a necessary conversation where they do not have all the answers. Many leaders feel they are expected to have all the answers, so when such a situation arises where they are unprepared, you might find them slinking away from handling it in a forthright manner. A good demonstration of this kind of boldness in practice is when leaders encourage a pushback from their employees and create an atmosphere for constructive debate where better answers are sure to surface.

A good leader always looks for opportunities to communicate, reinforce and share relevant information with others. When they are unsure about certain topics or problems, they are not shy to ask for opinion from their employees. Meanwhile, a bad leader tends to ignore or pass on the issues or problem to their employees. They hate having to solve a problem they are not familiar with; they are shy in asking for help and may feel it is wrong for a leader to ask someone from lower position for opinion.

It may seem negligible as a quality of boldness, but giving credit to others when so many leaders are image conscious and performance driven is an admirable, courageous trait. This is an exertion of honor among truly great leaders who accept the responsibilities of their positions by taking the blame for their team members and in giving them credit when success happens.

Here are some tips for you to become a bold leader:

- Be positive. Always seek an opportunity from each situation. From failures to mistakes, each situation teaches you something new. Mistakes are sometimes the most valuable sources of learning and help you to you grow.

- Speak out. Do not let your shyness get in the way of gut instinct. You need to speak out your thoughts, opinions, questions and answers to your team. Share everything you know and what you want to know. It is also a good way to learn and teach your team members.

- Identify risks. You should identify your risks and implement mitigating strategies. With strong self-awareness, you should be able to pick your battles by deciding what can be done and cannot be done.

Empathy

Empathy is the ability to put oneself in someone else's shoes is one of the traits of a good leader. Empathy is a big part of making executive decisions. This means, you can understand someone better if you view problems from their point of view. From there, you can figure out what caused their under-performance. Also, a leader who has a high degree of self-awareness is more likely know and be able to recognize how their decisions and feelings affect other people in a team.

Being empathetic does not mean that you are too sensitive or let emotions affect you - it simply means that you are able to visualize a situation or an outcome from a different standpoint.

The ability to see a situation from various perspectives is a virtually priceless asset. It is a part of what sets good leaders apart from excellent ones. The more that a leader is able to ascertain the viewpoints of his/her team members, the better equipped he/she becomes in maintaining compliance of the overall objective. The team will be more attentive because they will feel that their respect for the leader's guidance is reciprocated. If a specific task or process is having problems, you can try to work alongside a disgruntled team member, to better understand the person's point of view. Showing empathy in this way may take time, but you will often motivate the team member who you are trying to help. Not to mention other obvious benefits, but this will bring your working relationship closer as well.

Leaders who show empathy provide a sense to their workers of being heard. Workers who feel they've been heard gain self-satisfaction which they may then transform into a boost in confidence in their work and security among the workplace. Empathy elicits a tendency to work harder because those who receive it feel a stronger connection to the giver of it and may even feel they owe their extra effort to the leader as an expression of gratitude for being understood and respected. Empathetic leaders are also nonjudgmental, even when the feelings of others are in direct disagreement with their own feelings. They appreciate what the other person is feeling and understands how those feelings are affecting that person's perception, without passing judgment as to whether those feelings are right or wrong

Empathy is a great tool for building trust, and trust is a key factor in the smooth running of a team in business. Without trust, your subordinates will never willingly follow your approach or decisions. Being empathetic helps in achieving a good insight into a matter and thus, making better decisions. Empathy plays a key role in the retention of talent, particularly in today's information economy. Leaders have always needed empathy to develop and keep good people, but today the stakes are higher. When good people leave, they take the company's knowledge with them.

If your team members do not trust you, you are not a good leader but you are just a manager who does things just for your own benefits. A key component for building trust with others is empathy. When you show that you are aware of your team members' feelings and appreciate their feelings in an appropriate way, even when you are not agreeing with their opinions and thoughts, you win respect. This is how you build trust with empathy. The team members will have faith in you that you will at least take their feelings into consideration. You can then use this understanding of their feelings to then give your team members what they need to succeed, further strengthening your relationship, increase collaboration, to improve productivity and also generate more sales when you have happy team.

Without empathy, your employees will always have their guard up. They will always feel like they have to look out for their own emotional interest. While with an empathetic leader, the employee knows that their feelings will never be simply overlooked or ignored. Therefore, they will put effort into their tasks and consequently, it will increase productivity and profit.

A good way to increase your empathy in your team is to interact with them more especially outside the office. Many good leaders spend their time with their team members during off duty and holiday periods and they believe this is not only a good way to understand them better but also increase the closeness of their relationships by eliminating office politics, especially that which may otherwise exist between a manager and their subordinates.

Here are some tips on how to improve your empathy.

- Become an active listener - Empathy requires that you cultivate the trait of active listening. Personally, I strongly believe that most people are thinking how they are going to respond while the other person is still speaking. That is not a good way to listen. You may make a wrong interpretation. However, an active listener is totally focused on what the other person is saying. It helps you to interpret more effectively and efficiently the other person's view on the topic.

- Become curious about others - Highly empathic people (HEPs) have an insatiable curiosity about strangers. Curiosity expands your empathy when you talk to people outside your usual social circle, encountering lives and worldviews very different from your own. Many people are curious but few take the time or step out of their comfort zone to ask. Challenge yourself to slowly find out more about other people.

- Stand inside someone else's shoes – It means that you think from the other person's perspective or point of view. It is also like changing lives with someone. You have to do what they are doing to understand their actions and responses. For example, you can sleep with homeless to feel how homeless people survive through conditions where temperatures are lower at night, food and water and a good place to sleep are ongoing problems.

Charisma

Influencing people, making them obey your command, ensuring that they follow you - these aren't easy goals to achieve. Leaders should be able to invoke a feeling of motivation and awe in their subordinates, and that comes through charisma. It requires high level of Emotional Intelligence (EI), confidence, self-awareness and perhaps empathy and communication skills in order to be a charismatic leader.

Charisma involves a creative approach to tasks and to people. These leaders take creative approaches to everything including delegating tasks, solving problems, completing tasks, starting new projects or setting new goals. Charismatic leaders are those who thrive on innovation and often encourage their team members or employees to think "outside of the box." They want their team members or employees to be creative and innovative. The creativity and innovation demonstrated by charismatic leaders allows their employees or team members to trust in their capability of the leader. It requires the projection of oneself as genuine while being so well organized that that authenticity provides a welcome, fluid candor to every interaction. It is the idea that a professional may be so on top of their game that they make challenges look easy. We see it from star athletes in sports highlights, and in the workplace from people who radiate a kind of magnetism.

Having charisma lends itself to the idea that while a leader has organized and clarified a plan, he is monitoring the progress of the objectives and the members carrying them out. In forecasting future endeavors, he or she is able to maintain a comfortable attitude that is also invigorating for others, a feeling that can't help but influence others to feel better about themselves and their work. That is what we call motivation and inspiration. With good communication skills, a leader should frequently motivate and inspire their team members or employees. This encouragement can be compliments, money incentive or other reward or recognition.

Charismatic leaders are the ones who can be entrusted with turning a company around or going forward into unknown territory with a crack idea for a new product or new business strategy. They just want to take risks and stand out from the crowd. They want to lead their team or employees with them into the adventure as well. Taking risks and convincing others to take risks is a characteristic of the charismatic leader. They strongly believe on their abilities and also their team. The leader's high level of self-belief often results in successful risk-taking endeavors. A good leader views risks in an almost romantic way.

Charisma is supported by a strong sense of confidence that is so important to leadership, the kind that draws people to follow their lead and trust in their decisions even if they appear bleak at first. They possess a strong sense of self belief and rarely feel or express any doubt about decisions or goals made to him or herself and their team. They do not want to demotivate their team members or employees. They also know that if they step off this kind of confidence level, employees will start to have doubts and become demotivated.

This does not all just come from a feather in the cap though. Charismatic leaders operate with an internal system of highly strategical thinking, empathetic accordance with their associates and an eye for detail in reading their environment as well. They can then possibly use that information to their advantage.

To lead people, you must have a strong vision, which can capture the attention of people and unite them into working towards a specific goal. Good leaders entice their subordinates with suitable rewards and incentives and push them in the right direction. This is a crucial tool for every leader to build with. Without it you cannot build a vision.

To become a charismatic leader, it involves paying careful attention to the way you interact with other people especially your team members. To become one, you have to be confident, pay attention to detail and be assertive. Stay sharp and smart. If you're a charismatic person, you're usually less stressed, more successful and more attractive. That means you know how to look after yourself, and employees will notice your smile and you know how to look good without overdoing it. You are a leader in a team, you have to become a model in a company for your employees to follow and that means even in menial tasks.

Assertiveness

A good leader always has a dominant personality. Can you picture someone who makes decisions, and is easily swayed into changing them due to the opinions of others, in a successful managerial position? The answer is probably no. You can never envisage these unhealthy behaviors from a good leader.

How does a leader balance themselves between being assertive and pushy? They take the time to develop genuine relationships with team members. Ask about their goals in the workplace and what they would like to work on for themselves personally. Then good leaders will actually share a little about themselves, communicating what their own goals are and how they feel about changes. They engage in establishing a good rapport from the very beginning and maintain strong relationships. Later on, leaders will be able to use their influence within these relationships to delegate difficult tasks without meeting much, if any, resistance. Leaders and staff communicate frequently and everyone gives opinions, feedback and support to each other. There is no "us and them" encourage people to think of "Team" and "Teamwork".

Successful leaders will gather as much information as possible to gain a wide, clear perspective before taking action. Then, they will study and analysis the information. This sharpens their good judgment skills so they are perceived as levelheaded and fair.

Then, if their workers feel it appropriate to challenge their way of thinking, the leader can show grace by being open to discussion and allow better decisions to emerge, instantaneously winning their respect. They are flexible, encourage information sharing, and this can result in better decision making. However, a good leader is able to stick to their plan but they are open for their team members' opinions and feedback as part of the overall picture.

Another technique for ensuring that all the voices of your team members or employees are heard is for the leader to step out. Do not worry, it does not mean that you have to quit your job, but leave the meeting room. This can give your team participants a chance to speak openly, discuss options and make recommendations without making an effort to tilt in the direction they think the leader expects.

If a leader is keen on enforcing their point of view, then they must walk the walk, so to speak, to back it up. If they can prove their assertion by action and example, there will be no one to refute them. Consider in this way that when a leader comes off as curt, they may also be exacting a sense of transparency. Some people will appreciate the straightforward talk without candy coating the message. It is crucial for you to show your authority sometimes. You need to use your authority to make decisions when you think it is necessary to reduce any conflicts or misunderstanding.

Ross Elkins

In this sense, tactful communication becomes a prized element for an effective, assertive leader. If the leader can exhibit themselves in a range of emotions, even those such as frustration and anger, while maintaining professional respect for their employees, they will show themselves as being openly human. This quality, which is difficult to maintain within an authoritative position, goes to inspire those working for them.

A good leader is always firm in their approach to both decision making and their dealings with others. To evolve and perform as a leader in the business world, one must be assertive, and not a pushover. Make the decision to positively assert yourself. Commit to being assertive rather than passive or aggressive and start practicing today.

To develop your assertiveness, you have to value yourself along with your own rights. Understand that your rights, thoughts and feelings are just as important as everyone else's but remember they are not more important than anyone else's, either. Also, express negative thoughts and feelings in a healthy and positive manner and receive criticism and compliments positively. Lastly, learn to say "No" to things you are not willing to do.

Open to new things

Good leaders are always evolving, both in their outlook and the way they deal with things. A good leader is always open to new ideas, judgment, strategies and policies. An open, broad outlook on things inspires better decision making. Good leaders are always on their feet, thinking up new ideas, getting to know about the latest technologies, or plans that might help the business. The willingness to learn new things will manifest in your subordinates as well, as they look up to you, and the outcome will be a sharper and more efficient task force.

Bad leaders argue against open leadership style because it's a threat to their positions. They do not want to be replaced and wasting time to learn new ideas or things seems to them to be unimportant. Sometimes, they reject this as being an option because they don't know how to communicate in a way that opens up communication for others to engage. They do not have the necessary skill to communicate effectively to exchange information and knowledge with their subordinates.

Being open to new things also enhances your accessibility to different problem perspectives and may help you to get more insight about the problem. This gives leaders a better understanding and "pulse" on what is happening in the company or what kind of problems they are facing. It also eases the flow of information either directly or indirectly from your employees. In fast-paced industries, quick access to information is the key. It also allows you to lose your vulnerability and strengthen your skill set.

Here are some tips for you to improve your open mind.

- Learn something new. Broaden your knowledge and skills by educating yourself about other cultures, groups and customs. Try to see things from different angles and viewpoints.

- With new knowledge, go and hunt for new opportunities. You will notice that perpetually seeking and discovering new opportunities, new ideas, and new approaches to solve the challenges you face is often easier than other techniques.

- Meet new people. By meeting new people in your social network, it helps you to know different people from different cultures and backgrounds. It helps you to "open your eyes" and see their personalities traits.

- Openness starts within you. You need to learn how to think openly, speak without fear and shyness, adapt to changes quickly and be positive for any feedback.

Listening skills

"In some South Pacific cultures, a speaker holds a conch shell as a symbol of temporary position of authority. Leaders must understand who holds the conch—that is, who should be listened to and when."

- Max De Pree, American businessman and writer.

While it is essential that a good leader is assertive, it does not mean that they are obstinate about their decisions and do not even accept valid suggestions that might be useful to the business. A good leader is almost always also a good listener, as it is important to take your employees' opinions and insight into account. We listen to and obtain information and knowledge and this helps to understand and to learn.

Listening is the manager's most important leadership skill because it's really the doorway through which all the things that the manager wants from their team members happens. As the boss leads, listening to his team member is how he knows whether he's leading in the right direction or the wrong direction.

Listening is not only to improve your own leadership skills, but also increase your team members' commitment from it. You will gain their trust, as their opinion and feedback are listened to. Don't be fooled into thinking that being heard is more important than hearing. The first rule in communication is to seek understanding before seeking to be understood.

Listening to your employees' opinions can offer different perspectives that, even as the versatile and observant leader that you are, perhaps you have not considered yet. They may be able to enrich the dynamic of the workplace so that more employees are satisfied on a matter that you may have overlooked. They may be able to offer insight into troubleshooting or flagging problems with a business procedure or project stage that could save you and your company ample time and money.

Employees in the past have garnered great success for their companies because their superior has taken notice of them. The well-known story in the business world of 3M Company's stumble on the invention of the Post-it note is one such example. This has become the quintessential example of innovation for big businesses because although it happened all the way back in 1968 and took 12 years before it was actually marketed; there are very few other finer examples.

Spencer Silver, a chemist for 3M, was in the developmental stages of creating better adhesives. When he stumbled across a technology involving microspheres that formed a weak adhesive yet retained their stickiness so items could be pulled off and reapplied, he then had the trouble of finding a practical use for it. It was only after he got into talks with a coworker of his (Art Fry) that Post-it note development began.

Fry's problem was that he would bookmark his hymnal book for church choir practice with slips of paper, but when he went to use the book, the paper bookmarks fell out and he would lose his place. He remembered Silver's adhesive and began collaborating with Silver. Many other colleagues were doubtful that any success would come out of Fry's and Silver's developments together. They kept lobbying the idea until after extensive market testing in 1980, 3M released it onto the market. The Post-it was an instant hit – a product nobody thought they needed until they did.

An efficient leader is aware of the needs and grievances of his employees, and does not dismiss them when they feel the need to talk about something that pertains to the professional realm. An unwavering refusal to listen to employees would eventually lead to feelings of disrespect and loss of motivation. Paying attention o such grievances may lead to surprising advancements in company infrastructure, innovation development and even prevention of huge company losses or failure.

Here are few tips for you to become a better listener. Listen to be challenged and to learn something new. You should not waste your time worrying about what you're going to say to someone. Instead of that, you should focus on what's being said. Don't listen to have your opinions validated or your ego stroked, listen to be challenged and to learn something new. You're not always right, so stop pretending you know everything and humble yourself to others. Also, listen to both verbal and non-verbal communication. Body language speaks more than verbal language does. Pay attention to your speaker's body gestures, whether he or she is comfortable speaking with you or not or whether he or she is lying or not.

Besides, you also have to ask for clarification in detail if you are unsure or cannot understand. Probe the question asked by the speaker. It will show that you are truly interesting and paid attention in his speaking.

Lastly, you also should stand or sit facing your speaker and pay full attention. You should show them that you care about them. Sit straight or stand still facing toward them. It is also a sign that allows you to show respect as a leader.

Ability to deal with failure

Risk taking, corporate gambles and decisions that fall short of the mark are a part of being a leader. Sometimes your hard work just doesn't pay off. In such situations, a good leader is one who doesn't get rattled easily. A good leader is someone who is not discouraged or disheartened by failure, and chooses to focus on the next task at hand without letting their failures affect their judgment. It is crucial to learn from mistakes by treating them as an opportunity to grow better instead of just a lesson in failure and then putting the blame on someone else. It shows your unprofessionalism and degrades you if that's all you can glean from the situation.

Failure can occur in a number of places along the path of project investment and execution. A good leader should be able to pinpoint where along this spectrum a failure occurred and have the wherewithal to deal with it and/or learn from it accordingly so that it can be avoided in the future. Many senior leaders say that they have committed countless number of failures during their past experience. For them, failure is fueled the most rewarding opportunities and learning in their career. Whether it was the decisions made, the people they hired, the time spent on some problem or the result of their careless mistake, today it shapes them as a successful and good leader.

The key issue is the leader's capability to determine the root cause of a failure, going beyond transparent reasons for the problem. This approach may seem unnecessarily drawn out or tedious to others. A poor manager tends to blame the problem on their team members or employees and deduct from their wages without spending time to study and figure out what actually caused the failure. However, a disciplined leader will understand that the value of weeding out problematic root causes will ensure less future setbacks or roadblocks and more stable future successes. It is the difference of focusing on the short-term and on the long haul and, again, involves seeing the opportunity amidst the challenges.

A leader's attitude toward failure is a defining quality that should not only send the appropriate message to his or her subordinates to keep them from getting entangled in drawbacks, but should also shape their approach and expectations by keeping them aware of what exactly it is that they are pursuing. Bear that in mind when you're writing messages to employees or team members. Write in an appropriate way so your receiver will not be offended but they will take your messages into deep consideration for improvement. This helps everyone.

This means that for leaders in entrepreneurial ventures and research facilities, failure can be seen as a good thing because the information derived from a setback can be used to get closer to setting the right foot forward. At least they have found a way that could not work. It is now new knowledge for them. Thomas Edison said that he did not fail. Indeed, he had found 9,999 ways that could not work. In contrast, leaders in already well-established businesses such as manufacturing companies would more likely view a failure as some internal problem for which they are responsible.

Because so many employees, including those in mid-management and even executive positions, are reluctant to convey bad news to their superiors, failure can often go unnoticed until it is too late. They are afraid of taking all the blame and punishment. Stop that kind of leadership in its tracks. You should teach them, guide them and motivate them, as well as telling them it is fine to make mistake but you must learn from it as a lesson. A mistake is a past event; you cannot fix it nor travel back to fix it. That is why a leader who encourages his or her subordinates to highlight problematic issues immediately will be more successful than one who declares they do not want to hear bad news.

Admitting one's failures and not resorting to the blame game are marks of a good leader. Employees are more likely to follow someone who owns up to his mistakes and takes responsibility for them than someone who wastes precious time in mudslinging.

Here are few tips on improving your ability to deal with failure.

- Never take it personally. Separate the failure from yourself. There are many factors that caused a failure. Sometimes, when you have done your best, the project might also fail because of external factors. Do not give up! If you take it personally and give up easily, remember, Thomas Edison failed 9,999 times before he successfully invented the light bulb!

- Seek out opportunities for growth and learning. Failure is the key to success. Study your failure and every aspect of it and use it to grow stronger by not repeating it.

- Express your emotions after failure. After all the failures, you are still like the average person; you have feelings. You feel bad and it's all right to show that. You may lock yourself away or stay few days in bed or feel down after you fail but bear in mind that this state should never last longer than few days. Express your emotions; don't suppress them but bear in mind that you must rise again, having learned from the error made.

Chapter 2

What is Expected of a Good Leader?

If you are in a leadership position, there are a lot of goals for you to achieve, but no matter what the job is, the basic expectations from a good leader remain the same. It is said that recognizing passion, authenticity, integrity and ethics are the four cornerstones of an effective leadership. They become personal approaches learned and developed from applying oneself in a situational basis, not just from studying other leaders elsewhere.

It means that you must know yourself thoroughly and be unafraid to confront what you may not like in your approach. Only then can you find the foundation to lay these cornerstones and bring about an effective change to your surroundings.

Integrity

A good leader is one who puts the needs of the company above his, at all times. Integrity is a defining trait of a good leader. People tend to respect a leader who is devoted to the company and pulls all the stops out to make sure that the image of the company is not compromised at any cost. Honesty toward the company and the workforce is an endearing and rather appealing quality to have. A good leader will not only make decision to satisfy their board of directors, but will also pay attention closely to their subordinates for opinions, feedback and potential problems.

Integrity comes with a few affirmations that a leader must live by. Because leaders are essentially role models for the rest of the team – and not just their workforce, but also the company itself – it should go without saying that their word is their bond. That means they must follow through with their promises and think carefully about how they conduct themselves and their words to others. Once a leader makes a promise, they live by it. They should be responsible for the decision they have made and try to solve any arising problems with their employees, as more brains produce more solutions, ideas and knowledge.

A leader who breaks their promises or lies begins to plant seeds of distrust, doubt, and resentment in the minds of their workers. "Monkey see Monkey do", their employees who feel that distrust will also repeat the same thing. It is not just trust lost in their leader. Workers will lose their sense of commitment to the job. Eventually these leaders will reap what they sow when they see morale deteriorate, disharmony pervades in the workplace and efficiency begins to fall apart. Accountability is lost. Workers will lose respect for the company and either leave or slack in their job. These can cause a significant impact on productivity. This can also mean losing customers.

Cutting corners and cheating may have a temporary appeal for those tempted to take the fast track to success, although it is a short road and others will always catch on eventually. It becomes a case of not just failing oneself, but taking everybody else down too. In future, when you face the same problems or even more challenging ones, you will have trouble and difficulty overcoming them.

Telling the truth with consistency takes guts. It is not for the squeamish who are not able to confront people with bad news. It is important to be straightforward at all times and if at all possible, be prepared with a plan to counteract or bounce back from that bad news – with integrity of mission. A good leader has a clear mind to face any situation as it really is without twisting it or wishing it to be something else. It is called the reality principle.

Having the clarity to see a situation, good or bad, for what it really is, the grace to admit it to oneself and the integrity to keep everyone they are leading on the same page is what truly wins the loyalty of those working for you. They will be much more persuaded to get behind your course of action, provide constructive criticism and help find realistic solutions.

Good Communication

Imaging a scene you see on a beach. When you are walking around the beach and someone is calling you from the sea by waving his hand, is he greeting you or asking for help because he is drowning? The same goes for your office. You have to be a good communicator to figure out problems preventing you from achieving your goals.

"Email, instant messaging, and cell phones give us fabulous communication ability, but because we live and work in our own little worlds, that communication is totally disorganized."
- Marilyn vos Savant, world highest IQ human.

Previously we discussed the importance of good communication between a leader and their subordinates. Good communication involves not just speech, but also body language. Most business deals are cancelled because one of the parties get offended by the other's disrespecting behavior when they meet in face to face business meeting. You have to make sure that the messages your body gives off is the same message that you are intending with your words and your thoughts. Just as actions speak louder than words, body language is most often a dead giveaway as to what you are actually thinking and feeling regardless of your words.

Good leaders should be aware of their 'influence' as their body language is a critical aspect in influencing another person directly or indirectly. Good leaders should always bear their gestures in mind when communicating as the way they are seen affects both their personal brand and the company they are representing. The attitude they carry in their body language can be seen by everyone and can have a positive or detrimental effect on productivity within the workplace and outside world.

"Never forget that you only have one opportunity to make a first impression - with investors, with customers, with PR, and with marketing." Natalie Massenet, Net-a-Porter.

Body language plays significant role in first impressions when you are meeting with your clients or other people. Often, this is one of the most difficult skills that every leader has to deal with. They cannot control their body gestures while talking to the public or performing an important task, especially when they are suffering from stress.

Take note of your posture right at this very moment. If you are hunching, you have your legs crossed, you are folding your arms or basically making yourself smaller in stature, it is a telltale sign of introversion. These gestures also mean that you are defending yourself against something and are unwilling to talk with someone. You are closing yourself off in some way, and people take note of this even on the most subtle of subconscious levels. Poor posture and closing oneself off speak to lower levels of confidence and a lower sense of power. These are crucial especially when you are giving a public talk or news conference. Every gesture you make will be captured in images and they will become part of the meaning in a picture.

Conversely, open postures such as holding the hands on the hips, relaxing the hands behind the head, standing or sitting with legs further apart and so on are known as power postures. These natural postures establish dominance, one of the traits of a leader, and are even recognized in the animal kingdom. They exert a sense of confidence, engagement and willingness. If you get a chance to watch videos on successful leaders such as Obama Barrack, Bill Gates and Jack Ma, they will always face their palm openly and maintain a good posture in public and also inside the office. These postures are trained. Look for them on photographs and you are sure to see them.

Interestingly enough, studies have shown that by practicing these power poses for a given length of time, the body's physiology reacts to support a higher sense of confidence by an increase in testosterone levels in both men and women and a decrease in cortisol levels, which is a stress hormone.

Tests have been conducted by Amy Cuddy, a social psychologist, along with others, where people would be assigned to practice either high power poses or low power poses for five minutes before taking a high-stress job interview where they were recorded, judged and given no nonverbal feedback from the interviewers (blank stares). Coders, who were not aware which interviewees practiced which poses beforehand, then watched the tapes of the interviews and decided which people they would like to hire.

Sure enough, all the interviewees who had practiced the high power poses beforehand were chosen for hire and evaluated in high regard. The cause was not so much the content of their speech as it was the candidates' *presence*. The coders described them as appearing more confident, passionate, enthusiastic, authentic, captivating and comfortable – ALL qualities and traits embodied by great leaders.

This goes to show that while some people may naturally possess leadership qualities and others must work to achieve them, the engaging personal aspects of a motivating, approachable type of leader can be learned and practiced through these power postures as well as by other methods. You may need to put in effort in the beginning, but once you get used to it, it becomes your natural habit.

A good leader has a commanding personality, so make sure that you make good eye contact and adopt a firm handshake, among other physical gestures. Very often, it is the non-verbal physical gestures that form an impression of you in someone's head. Good body language is very important in terms of being a good leader. A quick tip for you is to always smile before a handshake or before communicating with someone.

You should avoid these gestures that often can be found in a manager.

- Showing strong signs of disagreement with sarcasm.

- Sitting with chair at an exaggerated angle away from (e.g. not facing) the speaker in a conference or meeting room.

- Fiddling with a pencil, pen or personal objects.

- Looking at other objects or the surrounding environment when talking to someone.

- Standing close or over others who are seated.

Here are some gestures you should practice to get a positive impression Respect the space of others and don't enter their office or workspace without permission.

- Lean forward in your chair toward a speaker

- Make eye-to-eye contact with normal blinking.

- Make slight nods of the head on key points made by speaker.

- Make little or no extraneous arm and leg movements while talking to others

Despite of that, you should also learn about other body language including facial expressions such as eye contact, breathing style, hand and leg gestures. These are essential to figure out what people think rather than what they say.

Analytical thinking

People in a decision making position of authority need to evaluate a problem from all possible stances before arriving at a decision.

Leaders must analyze the information they are provided with, and make key decisions only once they are sure about how these will affect the business right away and in the future as well. While making a decision, a good leader must consider other areas of business as well, so that growth is not severely hindered in a separate department. They have to think of the impact from production plant to front line customer services. Every stage is significant and contributes a lot to business operating expenses. If a leader fails to make an appropriate decision, it can lead to huge loss.

Leaders need to adopt a kind of 'Renaissance man' (or woman) attitude. They need to focus on becoming well-rounded and diverse in their capabilities and interests to increase the volume of potential resources and idea pools to draw upon. Lane Wallace of the *New York Times* explained that problem solving should be tackled from a multicultural platform, drawing upon academia, business, the arts and history.

When businesses focus is on crunching numbers alone, looking for profits, they leave out not just the critical thinking aspect but a sense of quality too. W. Edwards Deming noticed this and tried to persuade American businesses for years back in the 1940s to make some crucial changes about their attitudes in his 14 key principles for management. They refused to listen to him at the time, so instead, he was invited by Japanese business leaders to share his wisdom with them. After applying these significant components, he largely assisted in shaping Japanese business methods into what they are today – innovation moguls.

A few of Deming's outlined principles are as follows:

- Cease dependence on inspection to achieve quality. Eliminate the need for inspection on a mass basis by building quality into the product in the first place.

- Improve constantly and forever the system of production and service, to improve quality and productivity, and thus constantly decrease costs.

- Break down barriers between departments. People in research, design, sales, and production must work as a team, to foresee problems of production and in use that may be encountered with the product or service.

Leaders will not be able to expand beyond their current limits and see issues from multiple points of view without making the effort to dip their toes in first. To culturally expand their awareness, both in the company and in the world, they must adopt practices that encourage their education. Increase your network and begin establishing healthy relationships with the heads of other departments. As a leader of design for example, you will gain valuable insights by speaking with a leader in the sales department to know what specifically people are responding to and what they are not. However, with technologies available today, we can connect with our colleagues through emails, or in even faster ways such as internal communication tools, conference calls or via social media.

If you are working in an international company or even if you are not, speaking with employees of a similar sector from a different cultural background will provide a different way of thinking. A Japanese technician will think differently to a Californian one, and thus may be able to provide a solution where the other sees an obstacle. Travel and reading up on translated business articles will also assist in developing these alternative perspectives.

This becomes crucial if you are working for an international company. When you are required to travel a long way to a totally different country, you will need to learn how to deal with people from different cultural background. For example, Asian countries such as China, Japan, Korea and Singapore are Confucianism based cultures. You may find they only speak few words in two hours meeting, but they ask a lot of questions and give feedback, opinions and thoughts privately after the meeting. This is their cultural belief and it is called as "Giving Face" which means they respect someone who has higher social status or a higher position in a company. In past cases, some leaders cannot handle this situation and yelled at them to talk. However, at the end of the day, they did not realize the cultural differences and had their deals terminated right after their meeting as a result of their rudeness.

Your company product designers are the ones who sit in front of a computer to design the product for sale. But it is your sales and marketing department employees who go out to make deals with customers. So, they will have more valuable feedback directly from their customers than a designer who stays in the office every day.

By focusing on the larger picture, we can see what results happen as an effect of our direct efforts. Then by zooming in further to analyze individual components more closely, we can see how each department relates to another. We begin to understand the intricate relationships of complex business systems and better hone in on what went wrong and where as well as when it occurred. This further aids in our process of developing a solution because we will have gained insight as to how each department's decisions are affected by the other. That way, we can optimally come up with a solution that will benefit all departments and prevent future snags in the system as a whole. The system is intricate, and we must understand and respect it in that way to successfully work as a team. Always remember, you cannot succeed or achieve your dream alone, you need a team.

If there is a problem, a good leader must be able to figure out the root of the issue, and analyze the proper business processes in order to fix it. The solution to a problem must be such that it leaves no scope for harm to the company a few years down the line. Looking for quick fixes are sometimes the biggest reasons why leaders fail in their jobs. If their sales volume is dropping dramatically, they have to find out the problematic root from every perspective and departments within their company and their competitors. A leader should use analytical and creative thinking to find out and fix the problem within a reasonable time.

One other crucial aspect to take into account is the ambiguity of the business world. Because of globalization and the intricacies of business systems in supply and communication that were mentioned before, it is impossible to know everything that is going on and all the factors that add into the current problem being encountered. You must develop an attitude cavalier enough to not be too swayed by constant change where quick decisions must be made. It becomes a matter of considering all the available data, drawing upon a multitude of various resources including perspectives and people, trusting your gut instinct that comes with experience as well as allowing your better intuition to take over at times.

Here are some tips to improve your analytical thinking skills:

- Read books and study past case studies. Books are where you learn other people's experiences and knowledge. They might have spent years to gain the knowledge and experiences related within a book, but it only take few minutes for you to read and learn.

- Build your mathematical skills. Analytical and strategic thinking both require critical thinking to discover a problem quickly. Mathematic problems such as Souk, Monopoly and so on are great way to give your brain some exercise.

- Go for a walk and observe everything occurring all around you. Sometimes, we tend to learn more when we observe rather than when reading. You can observe how a homeless man or how a hardworking kid struggle in the street to find food and drink or income.

Consistency

In homage of this quality, consistency needs to be spread across the board, evident in everything a leader does. From punctuality, prioritizing, communication and feedback to emotional stability, integrity, ethics, empathy and assertiveness, consistency is a major asset to build strength, confidence and trust in yourself and those you are leading. If you keep on changing yourself either in decision making or changing goals, your employees will be easily confused about their direction to achieve the goals you set.

In order to stay on top of things and to show your team a sense of faith and reliability, a leader should almost always be the first person to arrive at work. It conveys preparedness and a jump ahead in the game that is crucial for competitively innovative markets. It will also provide you the time to get set up for the day so that you may make yourself more available to your team members later on who may have questions or need guidance. It should almost be implicit then that the leader is the last to leave. Hardly micromanaging, it is simply wise for a leader to make sure that at the end of the day, they know where their employees and their company stands. Before you leave your office, you can list out the tasks you are going to do for tomorrow. So, you can delegate the tasks to save time and you can go home to spend your personal luxury time without worrying what to do tomorrow.

You need to identify what is urgent, important, urgent but not important, important but not urgent. This can save a lot time to be delegated correctly on each task. Aside from that, it also helps you to delegate the unimportant task to someone else in your team. For example, replying to emails from other departments regarding some frequently asked questions is urgent, but no more important than preparing for a news conferencing session. For this, you can forward the task to someone else who has specific knowledge of how to handle the inquiry, freeing you up. It is also a way to give a chance to someone else to show that they are reliable.

Prioritizing tasks is the only way to stay organized and focused so that you and your team members can do what they need to get done. There will always be a list of things to do, as has been suggested above, and on the rare occasions when you or your team members may actually finish the expectations in that time period with room left to spare, there is still plenty of research and planning to do to keep your business moving forward. Keep lists and progress charts up to date and make a habit of knowing what needs to be taken care of next so you are not caught off-guard. And then, make sure that your employees are aware of that same information. This will ensure a greater sense of confidence in them because if they know that their leader is staying on top of things, they will be more motivated to do so as well without having to stress. They know and believe in their leader. If their leader asks them to do something unusual, they will do it without questioning their leader, because trust has been established.

Besides, as a leader, you should know how to delegate your project tasks to the right person and let him or her handle the task.

Communication, communication, communication. It's becoming a theme, isn't it? And it can't be emphasized enough. Your employees need to know how they are doing at their job. They need to know the results of their work so that they can use this feedback. They need to be able to know that they can come to you if they have a work-related issue or an idea to be able to pinpoint something that perhaps you were unaware of or had overlooked. You should be able to provide consistent encouragement for team members' commendable efforts, constructive criticism or corrections to mistakes or low-quality production on a consistent basis, and regulated updates for your team on how the business is doing directly from the right source. As stated before, it is crucial that a good leader should have those traits stated in order to perform their own tasks and also be able to help each other as a team. A good leader has to show commitment and pay close attention to the problems as they arise.

Consistency of integrity and ethics means that for the business or group venture, no matter what obstacles you face you must always, always stick to your established values without exception. FOCUS (Focus One Course until Success) is a simple yet powerful word for leaders who often switch between plans. They will not realize it costs a lot more than by focusing on one thing to do at a time. It will not only cause losses in profit, but also loss of trust from your team members. No cutting corners. If you begin to cut corners outside of the business, you will eventually notice the same short-handed practice from your employees within the business. "Monkey see, monkey do." If a leader started to lie, sooner or later, he will find out his employees will lie to him as well. Be the upstanding example, do something that can motivate and amaze your team members rather than reverting to showing off. It also means that you treat your employees fairly and consistently. If you choose to deny a certain privilege to one employee, do it across the board. It is your decision, but at least you will be consistent. Making exceptions or favoring one employee over another will attract disharmony and tension in the workplace. Never let your belief in political or cultural background or anything else for that matter, allow you to treat a team member unfairly. This means, never bring your own beliefs or thoughts into the office. This can cause internal conflicts easily.

Be steady in your assertiveness for the same reasons. You can present yourself in a friendly manner and still maintain an authoritative approach. Get rid of your bossy attitudes. If you let up because you don't feel like dealing with confrontation that day, you are giving your power over to that employee and they won't respect you for it, and then employees will catch on throughout the workplace. It is the idea that if you give them an inch, they make take a mile, so avoid giving that opportunity the chance. You hold the cards. Be fair. Make sure that you deal out your authority evenly for every employee including security guards or even a cleaner. You may receive something that you are looking for from them just as you might from a team member.

A consistent approach needs to be followed by a leader in order to ensure that the workers are motivated to act to their full potential. This is achieved by adopting various systematic processes such as delegation, fixing deadlines and providing feedback.

Motivation

The main purpose of a leader is to influence and motivate people. A good leader is one who sets an example for his or her team and acts like a role model and guide for them in times of need. Enthusiasm and loyalty is what motivates you beyond money or status. Strategies for effective leadership are discussed in the upcoming chapter, but what you need to know now is that one of the most desired qualities and prerequisites of being a leader is the ability to motivate people. In many ways, a leader is a visionary, and thus it is vital that they are able to convince people of the goal they need to fulfill. Some of the most effective ways for leaders to motivate their team members includes recognition, providing positive performance feedback where appropriate, and by challenging team members to learn new things. Recognition is when team members have their accomplishments recognized by others and then they will feel encouraged and appreciated for their efforts. Recognize your employees' contributions, big and small, with positive reinforcement. But keep in mind it's better to reward the effort than the person and if you overdo it or show that you have favorites, it can actually decrease motivation.

Prepare yourself before going into a meeting or when planning to speak with a specific employee. This will help you focus on what you expect from your team rather than what they are not doing right. You want to avoid putting others on the defensive. By precisely vocalizing what you are looking for, you will give a clear understanding for your employees to receive. By focusing on what you expect from them, you are inherently cultivating a more positive approach and avoiding traps like blaming or lowering others' self-esteem. This will also show you as a good communicator and listener. To practice, it is best to practice in front of a mirror, because it gives immediate and direct feedback to you.

Get people to think about their actions that they possibly haven't even considered by asking them 'why?' questions. Probe their statement when you are curious about them. Do not be shy. You must first be able to identify an issue specifically and then approach it objectively as an observation without making accusations. For example, ask, "Why do you think your number of sales has dropped this month?" Be genuine when asking. This shows empathy, which will help your employee, open up. Wouldn't you really want to know what's causing them to perform this way anyway? Once you get them to talk about it, turn the conversation toward focusing on solutions. Asking in a polite way will increase the chances to get real feedback from your employees than shouting or blaming them.

Tactics like asking solution-oriented questions are good motivators for discouraged employees because it puts power in their hands that they can work with. Allowing employees to come up with their own solutions gives them more space to manage themselves, providing them room to grow. When speaking with your team members, formulate your questions in an open-ended way that also directs them to come to a solution that you both can agree on. If you always get the answers you already know and not the ones you wanted to hear, you should spend more time to figure out how to ask questions that will encourage your employees to answer.

If you having issues in asking questions, especially if you ask in an inappropriate way, it will not only show your unprofessionalism, but also degrade your leader employee relationship, and create conflict and misunderstanding. This is an extremely important skill when you are working with a diverse cultural background company. Your language can mean something entirely different to those you speak to. Watch your words and body language every time you communicate. This is why many companies are trying to solve this problem but they never figure out what caused it in the first place.

Allow team members as much freedom to complete a set of clearly defined goals in the way that they want as possible. As long as you can be explicit with your expectations, giving team members leniency to tackle the job in their own way will keep them happy and help garner their loyalty to your company rather than a competitor's. Put them first, you second and your company third. This is a simple tactic yet it has been proven by research and studies that it helps to generate higher sales when you put your employees first. Build some facilities that can enhance their productivities such as a massage chair, table sports and perhaps a snack bar.

Permit casual dress at work for those who are not meeting with clients in person. Provide flexible work hours so that family people can attend their children's events or those who wish to hit the gym in the morning or sleep in just a little longer can do so. You might be surprised at just what a difference allowing people to be themselves in this way makes to their emotional wellbeing (which equals better performance at work) and sense of motivation.

Vision focused leaders are more appreciated than profit focused leaders. A leader has vision, but his or her team members may not have the same vision. This is because the leader may have better information and be able to stand back to think outside the box. The most motivational vision you can have for yourself and others is to "Be the best!" Many companies that cannot stand out from the crowd are like this because of employee apathy where leaders only see that their company is not the worst, rather than looking at what would make the company best. When your company product or service is the top selling product on the market, your employees will be motivated and encouraged as their efforts are paid off in good way. This is closely related to creating and selling a vision. You must be able to convince others to accept the objectives you have targeted. By emphasizing teamwork and recognizing that when people work together, you will be able to be a great leader.

Team members are also can be motivated when they are working towards personally meaningful goals. Attainment of those goals must require activity that is increasingly difficult, but attainable. In other words, people like to be challenged, but they must feel their goals are achievable to stay motivated. Besides that, you can also increase competition within the team.

Your employees can also be motivated by competition. That's because they will gain a certain amount of satisfaction by comparing their performance to that of others. This type of competition can occur naturally as well as artificially.

Responsibility

People who assume responsibility and do not shy away from it make for good leaders. A diligent leader is never afraid to accept extra responsibilities that others may not be willing to accept. However, responsibility oftentimes is a double-edged sword that can fall back on the one wielding it if they are not prepared to handle it correctly. It is important for you to keep your word once you have made promises. If not, it will destroy your reputation, trust and also impact your company image. As Warren Buffer said "It takes 20 years to build a reputation and five minutes to ruin it. If you think about that, you'll do things differently." Always think what the consequences are, if you do not take your responsibility carefully.

Let's talk power. As a leader, when you hear that word – power – it initiates some enthusiasm within you. Why else would you vie for a leadership position, right? It provides you the ability to realize big goals, to usher about change in the world, and it puts you in the driver's seat to control to an extent what direction that change takes the rest of us. This is known as Position Power. Some part of you, no matter how big or miniscule, is attracted to power. And so the question comes, when you search within yourself, what exactly drives your desire for that power, and how will you use it? Misusing it often known as abuse of power. Therefore, it is important for us to know our limitations and to have a strong self-awareness.

Leadership is all about responsibility; power is not. For the most part, power does not make one responsible. Responsibility is a composition of both innate and learned qualities within a person that we have discussed throughout this book, such as good communication skills, listening skills, consistency, the ability to self-motivate, integrity, focus and diligence. Power often illuminates these already-existing qualities or exposes the lack of them. If you lead with responsibility, progress can be achieved, but when it is power abuse, then only chaos and conflict follow.

Good leaders do what they say, and say what they do. They never say something if they cannot do or achieve it. These types of leaders are trustworthy, and show integrity. They get involved in daily work where needed, and they stay in touch with what's happening throughout the organization. Good leaders do not just sit in their offices, give orders and expect something from the team without leading them. A good leader demonstrates the actions and values that they expect from the team.

Even with high standards and polished integrity, leaders can and do fall short when it comes to exerting power and responsibility effectively. It can become too much and go to people's heads. In 1959, psychologists John French and Bertram Raven developed a structure for understanding different types of power and in the book, *What Keeps Leaders up at Night*, author Nicole Lipkin elucidates why it's important for leaders to know what type of power they are using. Knowing what type of power you wield will help you better manage it when dealing with people as well as focusing on the more sustaining attributes that provide affluent promise. A good leader knows his job and his mission, vision and goals clearly and can place them in one picture. Effective leaders manage performance by setting their expectations clearly and concisely. When everyone knows what's expected for his or her own tasks, it's much easier to get high performance. They can focus on clearly defined tasks.

Legitimate power is the type we may most often think of earning through promotions and initiative: it is when someone attains a high position, gaining control over others. It's important to know with this power that it was given and it can be taken away, even from founders, so it should not be abused. You have to understand what your limitations are and how people feel because of your words and actions. The pivot on which this power resides mostly has to do with the favor of the employees. If they trust you with it, they will approve when you exert your legitimate power. However, if you have risen to a position of power and your employees do not feel that you deserve it that can affect the whole company negatively.

Coercive power – power lead by fear and a certain kind of muscling in – should never be used. No one likes to be controlled. This is a dictatorship leading style, which will destroy creativeness and talent to be used effectively in your team. It will be a short-term power because you will lose respect and loyalty from your employees. No one will want to work with you. Even if they are willing to work for you, you will not be surprised by conflicts and chaos that occur regularly in your workplace.

Expert power comes from the experience and fine skills you have honed over the years, in association with reputable evidence of knowledge accumulated in education, most often in the form of a

Masters or Doctorate degree. In essence, you're smart, you know it, and you know how to apply it. That power is difficult to replace. Many successful leaders have priceless experience that only few have. Such as Jack Ma, he can influence someone in his team just with his childhood knowledge. They use their brain to talk and make actions, rather than their mouth. More importantly, people will pay you for it and will be willing to work with you or under you to continue supplying you with this power. No one can take this power away from you. The responsibility lies in the need to continue learning and improving yourself so that you can stay on top of your game and continue leading effectively. A successful leader such as Bill Gate reads books every night in order to gain more knowledge and get experiences in few paragraphs that somebody else has spent their whole life gaining from their experiences.

Informational power is short-term. Information is something you can easily obtain from your social connections, the Internet or a book. It will be spread quickly; you cannot keep it for yourself. It does not necessarily add credit to your reputation or encourage influence over others. It is the kind where once the information is shared, the power goes with it. We live in the information age. Competition sets businesses apart by weeks, so this kind of power does not last for long, and should not be considered for a long-term strategy.

The power of reward is found among those who are able to motivate people to perform in order to win raises, promotions and awards. According to Lipkin, people who administer performance reviews that determine raises and bonuses wield a certain amount of reward power. Everyone likes money and reward. They influence others to be more productive and effective in their jobs, which becomes a win for the company at large. When you set a prize either in a monetary form or position promotion or awards, your employees will work harder to achieve their desired prize. This should be hosted on either a monthly or annual basis. For example, life insurance companies that offer high reward to their employees who achieved their goals are likely to have unexpected sales as a direct result.

Connection power can be directly associated to networking. If you can develop the skills to create and maintain professional relationships with those in power, then you stand to be influential yourself. Building important partnerships with influential people puts you in a position to connect others with your network, which lends a great deal of power to you. A successful and good leader is also someone who is capable of building his or her valuable social network. They like to meet new people, as it creates new opportunity and new knowledge. There are several ways to expand your social network, such as Social Networking club BNI, online websites such as LinkedIn and through introduction by friends or family members. The responsibility here means that you must be able to appropriately judge the character of the people that you are linking into your network, because once you recommend them, their actions become a reflection upon you. Indirectly, it will establish an inherent trust and leader follower relationships.

Referent power is affiliated with the esteemed qualities and traits that were mentioned earlier on in this section – honesty, good communication, integrity, and so on. It is considered to be the most important and real power that leaders should embrace. It hinges on the development of quality relationships built with colleagues. It takes a lot of time, effort and hard work to build a good and trustworthy relationship with your employees. The power here is derived from people who admire and respect you, so your upstanding qualities become a direct influence upon them. You become the good leader by example, and can use this power to begin directing the course of action for your associates who rely on you. With this power, you can perform a task easier because everyone trusts you and your leadership skills. All you have to do is lead and they will follow. They will perform well in their task because they can focus on it.

The next time you think about that word, keep in mind that with great power comes great responsibility.

No bias

"Employees who believe that management is concerned about them as a whole person - not just an employee - are more productive, more satisfied, more fulfilled. Satisfied employees mean satisfied customers, which leads to profitability." Anne M. Mulcahy, Xerox

A good leader is expected to be completely unbiased. Leaders who show bias in the workspace create a disparity between workers, which leads to a noxious work environment. Such behavior is unhealthy for the smooth running of the business. A leader should also avoid their personal equation with a fellow worker that may cloud their judgment and decision making in their favor. As mention before, it is important to eliminate your personal thoughts and beliefs in your workplace. Get rid of your religious beliefs and discrimination from in the office. A successful leader leads a successful team and if you want to have that successful team, you have to create a strong team. A strong team is made up of professionals, trust, love, happiness, knowledge and so on. If you treat someone in the team unfairly, it is most likely that your team will not follow you for long, particularly if you bring personal belief into the issue.

This means taking cautious entrustment of the incentives that you provide to your team members, making sure that the origin of your desire to provide these incentives comes from a business standpoint and not a personal one.

Why is the phrase, "It's not personal, it's business," so commonly heard? Even though it is taken out of context sometimes, this expression reiterates purpose of action in the workplace. Sometimes the managerial decisions that have to be made as leaders are very difficult ones. One bad apple can ruin the whole barrel. Leaders must value their employees and realize that it is successful employees that make a company successful, however the leader must ultimately do what is good for the business. This means giving a promotion to the right person for the job and not to someone just because you are on friendlier terms with them. When you are making decision regarding promotion, award or any decision that can directly affect your employees and the company, one solution is to ask a third party to give advice.

Even though personality and work performance may be intertwined, a leader's conduct with employees must always lean toward work performance. You may find certain aspects of an employee's personality irritating for example, but it would be erroneous to criticize them unless it was directly affecting their work, other people's work around them, or violating certain ethics of the company. And it would be a waste of time on the leader's part to try to make the facts fit the theory.

A good leader must practice emotional stability and separate their personal judgments from their professional ones within the company, seeing everyone objectively to guarantee fairness.

Self-Assessment

Good leaders are consistently taking stock of their shortcomings and personal strengths. They like to question their strengths and weaknesses, in order to always stay on top of the game. They choose to categorize their abilities and their shortcomings in order to assign tasks to their workforce better by evaluating the strengths of the employees and deciding who would be perfect for the job. A good and successful leader is one who wants to grow better every day. They never stop learning, as learning is lifelong habit.

To make sure you have strong self-assessment about your strengths and weaknesses, you can ask direct feedback from your team members in face to face communication. Compared to digital communication, such as emails and messages, face to face communication is best way for you to get honest feedback and if someone is lying to you, you can spot it easily by reading his body gestures or body language.

Good leaders do not rush recruitment, and hire people who complement their skills. Meanwhile, they work on their weaknesses to become better workers and more productive to the workplace. Hiring an employee costs more than giving training to an existing employee. Usually, it takes months for a new employee to get used to the company's environment and working procedures. Instead, you should give appropriate training to your employees especially to improve their weaknesses. Working on their weaknesses also provides the opportunity to see the world around them from a different standpoint, which opens the door to more insightful opportunities. They remove the ego from their perspective so they can see their actions and thought processes and others' with an objective lens.

This type of vision helps leaders also bring a sense of honesty to the workplace that may seem uncomfortable to share at first. However, as workers see the leader applying the same principles to themselves, they will gain incentive to be more open to this ongoing process.

The more objective a leader can be with themselves, the more that they can do so with others and by nature show others how to do it for themselves. It goes to show that focusing on weaknesses is not a horrible or cruel thing to do because it offers the gifts of potential growth and brings a shared sense of humanity to those who are open to it. Team members and their leader can then better support each other, knowing directly where to apply that support. This in turn will enforce a sense of togetherness that will help build the strength of the team as a whole. Similarly, if you are in a car convey, all of your members know where their next destination is, so everyone can drive to the destination without getting lost. One thing you have to focus on is your members' vehicle status. When one car breaks down, everyone will stop to give help. The convoy will not continue until the car gets fixed. It is all about team spirit and willingness to help each other to achieve a shared goal.

Introduction to the Enneagram

The Enneagram (pronounced: ANY-uh-gram) is a prolific symbol of ancient alchemy (the science of transformation) that is over 5,000 years old, although its exact origins remain unknown. While its application has been attributed to many spiritual practices, the Enneagram, "ennea" meaning nine, has provided a very lucrative and practical use in the business world.

The Enneagram illustrates nine different personality types that together comprise a single unit, and has been used worldwide to assist business managers and leaders in forming optimal work teams for collaborative efforts and project execution. It has helped assess which employees are the best in working together and determine which employees are best for the job in working on specific projects.

The nine personality types and brief descriptions of each are as follows:

1 – The Reformer is best known as perfectionists, responsible, fixated on improvement

2 – The Helper (Mentor) is best known as selfless, socially aware, extrovert

3 – The Achiever is best known as hard-working, competitive, focused on the presentation of success

4 – The Individualist (Designer) is best known as identity-conscious, unique and individual

5 – The Investigator is best known as thorough, perceptive and proactive

6 – The Loyalist (Troubleshooter) is best known as engaging, diligent and likable

7 – The Enthusiast is best known as creative, future oriented and open minded

8 – The Challenger is best known as self-confident, decisive and practical

9 – The Peacemaker is best known as harmonic, accommodating and reassuring

What is unique about the Enneagram is that it recognizes the spectrum of personal qualities, from the basic characteristics of each personality type, to when each type is at their best and when they are unhealthily placed as well, affected by factors such as prolonged stress. In this way, one can use this system to help identify their own strengths and weaknesses as well as that of others.

A good leader would be able to make great use of this tool not only to identify their own shortcomings and work on improving them, but also efficiently delegate tasks and workloads to the right people. As a leader should always be seeking out ways to boost morale and help improve their workers' individual skills, one can apply the knowledge of the Enneagram to assign certain jobs to team members that will stimulate their growth.

That aside, this is a tool that helps them to delegate their task perfectly to their team members or employees. They know who is good at what and why they are good at something.

Chapter 3
Hard Power & Soft Power

Leadership styles are changing drastically as time progresses. We no longer live in a world where a well-oiled organization or institution was thought to be one that used a hierarchical, command & control style approach to solve its problem. Simply put, they no longer work anymore. Flow of information is of paramount importance in today's age and such hierarchies simply hamper fluidity which is not something companies can afford. Going a little outside of the business model, even the Pentagon reports that army drillmasters are instructed to play more of a counselling role and less of a "shouting role"! The world as a whole has undergone an evolutionary and participative process that has become more catalytic in the past decade.

The information revolution has affected all fields of life, ranging from politics to businesses. The phrase knowledge is power applies more to this current age than it ever did. Hierarchies are becoming flexible and are being embedded with a network of contracts. Knowledge workers have to be lured in to keep them motivated using different incentives compared to the traditional industrial worker. A number of polls conducted in advanced countries have showed that people have become quite less deferential to authority in both organizations & politics. The classic economic theory that firms can be split into hierarchies and internalizing functions is being replaced by a notion that firms need to be networked and outsourced. Compare GM to Toyota respectively. And in order to successfully manage such organizations, leadership needs to select people who are talented, can be trusted and navigated through the use of soft power.

Leadership experts are increasingly reporting success of a technique that many would term as a "feminine style of leadership", and in a way they won't be wrong. Talking in terms of gender stereotypes, a male style of leadership is considered as assertive, autocratic, competitive and most of all commanding. In contrast, a feminine style of leadership is considered as cooperative, integrative, participatory and aimed at tolerating the behavior of her employees. A 100 years ago, there weren't a lot of women in corporations and businesses let alone, in the top leadership positions. But with the passage of time as they fought their way to the top, they had to adapt to the masculine style of leadership but this was seen as a direct contradiction to their female "niceness" which didn't resulted in a lot of wins.

Enter the information age and the previously known "feminine style of leadership" is exactly what stakeholders are looking for when they're thinking of handing their organization to someone. Even men had to learn these skills and lead in a more "nice" manner in order to be seen as great leaders by their followers. Nowadays, leadership is seen as more of something that deals with encouraging employee participation compared to something that means issuing commands to subordinates. It is being seen that soft power is the ultimate quality for leadership.

But wait! Aren't the greatest Silicon Valley inventors' jerks? Stanford psychologist Roderick Kramer has said that the world shouldn't rely too much on soft power skills and should focus on hard power as well if they truly want results. He cited most billionaires, politics and other leaders to support his cause. And in a way he is right; too much of anything can't be good. A good balance is necessary and that is exactly what this chapter will teach you.

Most of the skills that are required for a good leader are mentioned in the previous chapter so they won't be explained with much detail here.

The New Way to Get the Job Done

No matter what anyone says, leadership and power are inextricably connected. In a nutshell, power is one's ability to affect the behavior of others so that one may get what he wants. Generally, there are three ways to do so:

1. You can coerce people with threats,

2. You can make them do something by making hard payments,

3. You can attract them and use a softer approach,

Soft power is based on the fact that the preferences of others can be altered through enough work at a specific angle. At a personal level, you will be quite aware of the power held by attraction & seduction. For instance, in a relationship or marriage if the wife wants something done, she doesn't pay or intimidate her husband into doing it! In a similar manner, power doesn't always rest with the breadwinner of the family!

Smart executives are well aware that leaderships doesn't mean issuing commands and waiting for them to be implemented in one way or another. Instead it also means leading by examples and attracting others by cooperation. A multinational organization cannot be run by threats & intimidations alone; if that's what a leader does then soon there won't be anyone to lead. Your power on the other hand would be much greater in magnitude and useful if you can "sell" your vision to your employees in a charismatic manner.

The ability to establish others' preferences is linked with assets that can't be touched like personality, values and vision; in the end these traits will have more power than money or firing threats. If a leader has a clear vision, shares it with his followers and values others' opinion on it, then there is a greater chance of the entire venture costing less compared to a leader who is autocratic in nature. Soft power is basically the power held by a leader to attract others without the use of threats, coercion or any other intimidating factor. In terms of resources, the only thing required for a person to utilize soft power is a personality & vision.

There are various ways through which employees can be attracted. Many are drawn in to others by their inherent qualities and the way they communicate their vision. This particular attractional quality is known as charisma which many refer to as a mystic power one holds over a group of people whenever he is present. And remember, communications don't always have to be literal; they can be symbolic as well. When any kind of communication consists of a large amount of emotion then it is known as rhetoric. Some communications are willfully designed in such a manner that they won't give others a chance to speak while others require input from others in order to go on. It will be up to you as to which one you want but ultimately the organization will flourish if you act according to the situation.

Coming to Hard Power, the two main techniques that govern it are threats & inducements which are quite linked. You might think that inducements, bonuses or rewards are something that would make Hard Power attractive but in fact their removal makes up for a threat that has a direct effect over employee behavior. Therefore, Hard Power isn't as good as you might think it is.

The following table will help you understand the difference between Soft Power and Hard Power:

Types of Power	Behavior	Sources	Example
Soft	Attracting & co-opting with others	Personality and communica tion	Charisma, persuasion
Hard	Threats and inducements	Intimidatio n, rewards, etc.	Hiring, firing, promotions, compensation

Hard Power and Soft Power may be different but a company or any organization cannot survive if both of these don't work in conjunction, according to the situation. Sometimes for instance, people are attracted to hard power because they believe in some kind of myth about the individual leading and think that they can excel by simply following orders. These extreme cases are a fact and are better known as "the Stockholm Syndrome" which was meant to define prisoners who become attracted to their captors to reduce painful stress. Therefore, sometimes even great intimidators can kick-start peoples' productivity and result in success and implementation of the leader's vision.

Sometimes Hard & Soft Power interfere with each other while sometimes they reinforce them. Almost every leader must possess a certain degree of both if he wishes to succeed. Even in the past, no one man has been able to coerce everyone around him using nothing but intimidation. Even the cruelest of dictators had henchmen who held a significant amount of influence over others in order to impose the ruler's orders. Even Hitler and Stalin had such a circle and didn't dictate each and everything that went on. Machiavelli stated that it is better to be feared than to be loved but we forget that the opposite of love is not fear, it is hatred. And hatred is something even Machiavelli advised against. Whenever hard power undercuts soft power, the leader is put in a difficult situation. The best example is that of United States that has been trying to eradicate terrorism either through invading countries or by handing out cash (AID!) to other countries but the results haven't been groundbreaking at all and seeing the current situation of the world, I would say the conditions are much worse.

What is the solution then?

The solution is combining the two powers and forming what is known as "Smart Power".

Soft Power is not always good and is not always better than hard power, if that's the impression you're getting. Remember, you might have to deal with clever, egoistic employees who don't like to be manipulated by sugar-coated statements. In this case, you'll need to flex your hard power muscles and use them; you'll either have to threaten the employee with demotion or a weekend at work or have to coerce him with cash prizes. Like any form of power, Soft Power can be used both for good as well as for bad purposes. Remember, it's not always better to twist minds than to twist arms!

For instance, I may want to steal your money. I can do so by either persuading you to give me the money so I can save the world or by simply pointing a gun at you. The first case may save you from getting injured but the end result in both cases would be theft which is wrong.

Transformational & Transactional Leadership

When used wisely, Soft Power can translate into a set type of leadership known as Transformational leadership. This form of leadership is fed on charisma and is based on the fact that charisma can get anything done. Charisma has been mentioned in the previous chapter but I'll explain it once again; it is basically the quality of an individual's personality by which he can make others believe in his vision. Others might see the person as someone with exceptional, superhuman powers! However, charisma is not something that's static, in fact charisma builds up with the passage of time and is heavily dependent upon recognition from others. In other words, Charisma has both a sociological dimension as well as a psychological one. An example of increased charisma is that of Hitler who accomplished a string of political victories in the 30s which raised his charisma to a very high level, one that would turn into over-confidence and lead him to war. As his charisma rose, his number of followers increased as well but as he started losing the war, they shrank in size. This means that a leader will have a hold over his employees for as long as he keeps the organization profitable. A decline in the success rate would mean a decline in the number of followers.

The Business Press has noticed similar reactions from many CEOs. They term CEOs as charismatic whenever everything's going their way but as soon as they lose something like an acquisition, etc. the press terms them as non-charismatic. In May, 2000 John Chambers of Cisco was termed as the best possible CEO ever but after a year when the market declined by $400 billion, he was termed as naïve. And the most important thing is that stakeholders and board of directors look for such CEOs who have an excellent, charismatic public profile that could increase their profits by many folds.

Leadership theorists often use the word "charismatic" to define a process that relies on inspirational power resources instead of assumed power that comes from holding a position of power, e.g. CEO, President, Minister, etc. Leaders who are charismatic are excellent at communication, clear in their vision and confident, managing each of the impression they create. The following are a few types of leaders who are termed as charismatics:

- Close Charismatics – these individuals work best when put at the command of a little group,

- Distant Charismatics – they rely on a remote performance rather than a one-on-one discussion,

- Socialized Charismatics – these people use their powers & skills to benefit others,

- Personalized Charismatics – these are more self-serving and have a narcissistic behavior,

But regardless of the type of charisma a person holds, it is extremely difficult to know one's true intentions in advance. One study showed that charisma is valued more when a person leaves the organization rather than when he is in-charge of it.

It is also a fact that followers are much more likely to see a leader as charismatic when they are most in need. For instance, in 1939 Winston Churchill was not seen as a person holding charisma and was known as a back-bench MP. But within a year, his vision and communication skills along with the current requirements of time made him Prime Ministers with the entire nation supporting him. However, in 1945 when the public focus turned from war to the construction of a welfare state, Churchill lost and was no longer seen as charismatic. So you see, charisma isn't something you can conjure; there are several factors that directly affect the amount of charisma one holds.

In the 1970s and the 80s, leadership theorists derived the concept of transformational leadership from the value of charisma. It was stated that transformational leaders are those leaders who use their powers for a positive change by appealing to their followers'/employees'. They incite values that are positive like kindness, support, motivation instead of fear, hatred and greed.

On the other hand, transactional leaders are those who motivate their followers by feeding off their self-interests. Where transformational leaders show qualities that are good for the entire organization, transactional leaders get the job done by targeting the individual they need to. Therefore, conclusively transformational leaders rely more on a softer approach whereas transactional leaders are heavily dependent on their hard power.

Transformational leaders give away their self-interest in favor of collective benefits to the company as well as its employees. Therefore, an employee working under a Transformational CEO is much more likely to get inspired as well as motivated to take on challenges compared to an employee who has been ordered from a Transactional CEO. Transformational leadership also integrates an element of intellectual stimulation which broadens employees' awareness of the current situation of the company. Basically, transformational leaders share most of the company's details with their employees to keep them in the loop. This gives them a better picture of reality which triggers an honest response in return.

On the other hand, transactional leaders are more concerned with getting the job done one way or another and therefore set concrete milestones & incentives for their employees which are otherwise replaced by threats if the work is not completed in a timely manner.

But just as hard power complements soft power, these two types of leadership are related to each other as well. It would be best if leaders combine these two approaches and pick from a menu of hard & soft power skills to lead the organization. Jack Welch who worked at GE described that in his early days he had to use considerable hard power and top-down approach to restructure the company. However, once the transformation was done, Welch soon changed his leadership style and became an emotionally intelligent leader with charisma as the major weapon.

A leader may use both hard & soft power skills to achieve his transformational objectives. In democratic organizations, force is not an option so the only hard power resources left are either coercion or inducements, e.g. bullying, buying, hiring, bargaining, etc. On the other hand, the key soft power resources available to a leader are charismatic attraction, emotional inspiration through communication and persuasion through kindness. A CEO of a newly merged firm will find it very hard to integrate one company into the other if he uses the hard power approach of firing anyone who comes in his way. In such cases, a soft-power approach is extremely important to attract people and get them onto your vision's bandwagon.

We can use the term transactional style to describe what leaders do with their hard power and inspirational style to describe what they do with their soft power resources. Combining these two resources and using them produces a unique 2x2 matrix. An example of such a matrix along with Presidents that fall into the respective category is as follows:

	Transactional Style	**Inspirational Style**
Transformational Objectives	Harry Truman	Franklin Roosevelt
Limited Objectives	Dwight Eisenhower	Bill Clinton

In fact, such a way of representing leaders is easier to the one-dimensional approach as most leaders should & will adopt to multiple styles of leadership instead of one. In any event, the key to success would lie with the way the leader combines his soft & hard power resources. When these two powers are combined they give rise to "pragmatic leaders". The best example is that of Benjamin Franklin who wanted to change the status quo but didn't achieve such a change through his charisma; instead he formed elite network of alliances that worked in conjunctions, behind the scene to get the job done.

When talking about transactional leadership, it is more likely to be effective in predictable environments. The reason behind this is simple; stable organizations often aren't looking for change and are happy with their growth patterns. Therefore, they will look for leaders who would use the existing mechanisms (incentives) to run the company. In contrast, a turbulent company that is on the verge of collapse is more likely to elect or hire a charismatic leader who can use his mystic powers to drive the company out of crisis!

Hard & Soft Power Skills

We've talked about various situations in which hard power & soft power can be applied both individually and in combination. But what are the precise skills that leaders need to combine to channel their "Smart Power" instead of relying on a single variant. You'll find the details of these skills given in the previous chapter; over here I've only given a basic overview:

The following three skills are more closely related to soft power & a transformational approach.

- Vision – simply put, it is the ability to conjure an awesome & inspiring picture of the organization's future. The CEO of Federal Express said that the primary task or challenge that a leader faces and must have his focus on is to communicate his vision to the organization's employees.

The vision should not only attract the top-tier management or a specific set of employees but should consider each and every employee of the organization. It must provide an effective diagnosis of the problems faced by the company. Anyone can judge the level of a leader's vision by judging whether it creates a balance between risk & realism or not and whether it takes under consideration people's capabilities & skills when setting up goals. Remember, any person in the world can produce an ambitious wish list as to what he wants with his company but only a leader can decide whether his employees will actually be able to handle the milestones.

- Emotional intelligence – this is a leader's discipline, self-mastery and empathic capacity that allows them to direct their personal passions & charm their way into their employees' mind. Emotional intelligence is vital in determining the consistency of a leader's charisma and must be authentic in order to have a permanent effect over the organization. You must understand that emotional intelligence will also require some external effort, i.e. acting if you want to successfully sell it to your employees. One noticeable example is that of Ronald Reagan who was an actor before coming into politics. When any leader wants to get financial results out of his organization he must begin with his own life first so that he can conjure up the right emotional reaction. Once the employees notice a calm temperament in the leader's personal life, they're bound to follow him in professional life. Humans like all other animals focus a lot on their leaders so it's the leader's responsibility to control any signals that may prove harmful to his organization.

- Communication – An attractive leader must also have the capability to communicate effectively. Communication is the building block of almost every profession and is vital for growth. A leader needs to communicate using his words, symbols, body language and personal example. Winston Churchill often related his own success to the mastery of English language. However, excellent rhetorical skills are not always necessary for success. For instance, Mahatma Gandhi didn't have excellent speaking skills; however he led by personal example and was undoubtedly a great leader. Having great organizational skills which is the ability to attract & maintain a skilled inner circle is also vital for a leader and can even compensate for a wide communication gap. Having a trusted inner circle means the leader does not need to address every single division of employees; instead he can address his inner circle and communicate his vision right down to the bottom. Harry Truman is a perfect example of a leader with poor communication skills; however where he lacked in rhetoric, he had excellent set of advisors which made his presidency such a success. Leaders can also communicate quite effectively using symbols, actions and example which can make up for poor speaking skills.

Two skills in particular, given below are more inclined towards hard power and a transactional style of leadership.

- Organizational capacity – this is a leader's ability to successfully manage the structure of the organization and set the reward systems in a manner that would actually get the work done. The three words that are most closely related to organizational capacity are hiring, firing & compensation. The management of flow of information is extremely important as not every employee should have sound knowledge of the workings of the company. Leaders must pay special attention when managing their inner circle so that only targeted information gets out. They should equally focus on inputs coming from the employees and shouldn't become too used to compliments. He should expect criticism from his employees and should notice a trap if they don't come in after regular periods of time.

- Political skill – politics is everywhere whether it's home, classroom, or a workplace. It is of paramount importance and shouldn't be skipped by any leader. Politics can be in a number of forms namely, manipulation, intimidation and negotiation. The skill is related to hard power however sometimes it can rely on soft power skills like inspiration, developing trust, motivation, etc. Having political intelligence means that you can size up the weaknesses and insecurities of others at any point to get them to agree with you. This may be an evil thing to do but sometimes is necessary especially in corporations where politics surfaces at every point.

Sometimes it is necessary to throw others off balance using a calculated loss of temper to show them your dark side. This will induce a fear in employees that there can be consequences to their actions which can make a transformational leader more powerful. This is one example of combining hard power with soft power to form smart power. Margaret Thatcher for instance always portrayed herself as a "know it all" even when she didn't which helped instill intimidation in her advisors and followers.

In many cases, a leader can get the job done after his soft approach has failed by showing a dark side to himself however at some point he would need to readdress the issue otherwise the bad behavior would eventually catch up to him and lead to a brain-drain. In centralized institutions and organizations hard power can often overtake soft power resources however in decentralized and shared organizations hard power can often lead to resentment and lesser control therefore, a combination of both is required to deal with such issues.

By now it should be clear that hard power is not better than soft power and vice versa. It's all about perspective and context. It is vital that a leader knows how to combine his tools and form a well-oiled machine rather than shifting gears all the time. To deal with, a sixth crucial power known as Contextual Intelligence is formed which is basically a person's ability to combine his hard & soft power skills to form a smart leadership pattern. It is explained below:

- Contextual intelligence – this skills is basically defined as the ability to recognize an evolving workplace in order to get the most out of the company. The skill is widely used to reorganize firms depending on the market pattern however in a broader sense, the skill is actually an intuitive one which helps an individual align or realign all his resources depending on the workplace and his employees need. It involves going with the flow rather than against it without the employees knowing it, otherwise it can turn into extortion. When a leader uses his contextual intelligence he uses his hard power, soft power or smart power skills according to the current situation rather than relying on common patterns. A leader for instance must understand the importance of some core employees without which the company cannot function and should keep on enticing them with offers from time to time so that they don't leave. This may go against the basic rules of transformational leadership but some employees are more interested in benefits rather than charisma.

In addition, the leader must understand strengths & weaknesses of different individuals in the company and shape them in such a manner that they can be exploited as a "last resort". The individuals should also be aware that their weaknesses are no longer a secret however they shouldn't get the idea that you'll be trying to use them otherwise they may start planning a full blown resort. Just the idea of insecurities gone public is enough to keep someone working. One of the most rigid institutions in the world, the US Army tries to train its officers so that they respond to every environment differently rather than using a hammer to kick through every door. This should give you a good enough example of how the world is changing.

The following table summarizes Soft Power, Hard Power and Smart Power skills in once place.

Soft Power			
1.	Vision	i.	Attractive to followers
		ii.	Balances capabilities & objectives
2.	Communication	iii.	Words, symbols & example
		iv.	Persuades both inner circle and distant followers
3.	Emotional intelligence	v.	Ability to manage & conjure charisma
		vi.	Emotional control & self-awareness
Hard Power			
1.	Organizational capacity	vii.	Manage information systems & rewards
2.	Political skill	viii.	Ability to bully or buy your way in,
		ix.	Maintaining coalitions & allies
Smart Power			
1.	Contextual Intelligence	x.	Acknowledging evolving environments,
		xi.	Capitalizing on current trends,
		xii.	Changing governing style according to needs.

Contexts & Leadership

Up till now, we've come to the conclusion that context overrides all so if context rules all then how does it relate to a person's skills? Contextual intelligence is heavily reliant on exercising one's political skill however it is much broader than simply focusing on one's weakness & strengths and exploiting them when the time comes.

The first thing that every leader must focus on is the current political atmosphere of his followers. He must understand how political culture is dependent upon power sharing and how people can be convinced to follow the leader. For instance, an army general faces a much different political atmosphere compared to a university chancellor. Similarly, a government runs in a different manner compared to an NGO just as an armor division doesn't work the same way as a social club. Even similar organizations have different political atmosphere; a software company has a much different political atmosphere compared to an open-source community.

The political situation helps a leader realize his limits as well as the magnitude of power he can apply to his followers before facing resentment. It also gives him a clear idea whether he can switch to transactional style of leadership or transformation style.

Leading individuals who consider themselves leaders is much different than commanding troop who have been taught to say "yes" to everything. The first step in recognizing the political atmosphere is realizing whether you're running a hierarchical organization or a flat company where everything isn't always top-down. For instance, in Senate a politician needs to develop wide political consensus with fellow senators and agree to many of their demand which he might deem unreasonable however as president he can often use his own Veto or Presidential Ordinance to get the job done without any hassle. Generally, people working in flat hierarchies need to work on their political skill a lot and need to assemble coalitions more than people working in centralized organizations.

An organization's standing, i.e. whether it's publicly owned or a private entity often has a strong influence over its workplace culture. Moreover, a private company would often have more resources and independence compared to a government institution which gives a leader greater control over his followers. Any public company's leadership finds it very hard to use pure hard power to get the job done as even the slightest hint of intimidation can sometimes lead to human rights cases. On the other hand a private organization's CEO can hire or fire any employee without any notice (in most cases) which means he can flex his hard power muscles more often. Private companies are also more efficient than public ones and an organizational changeover can be easily made without filing a lot of paperwork. It has been frequently found that successful business leaders fail whenever they go to government organizations due to lack of understanding of the diversity.

Another extremely important aspect of contextual intelligence is the ability to stay dynamic rather than following a single policy. Everything changes with time including the employees' demands so the leader should keep on working to keep the status quo from tipping by keeping his employees at all times. Almost always, people are looking for change which is also one of the biggest reasons for a leader's downfall. The leader should acknowledge this need for change and take steps to ensure the people it's happening. Mostly, people are looking for greater autonomy depending on their service for the company which can be rewarded by giving shares to the person. This will make the person feel important and an integral part of the company, which will thus keep him motivated towards your goals.

Leaders also need to assess the situation and analyze whether hard power will be welcomed or resisted. Situations which invite hard power takeovers are known as "autocratic situations" whereas a leader who always uses hard power to solve a problem is known as "autocratic manager". There is a distinction between the two and no leader should be a complete autocratic manager otherwise his downfall would be imminent in the near future. A leader can truly excel if he is both participative and autocratic, knowing when to use which property to get the job done. Many employees want a certain degree of autonomy when doing their work, e.g. financial handling of a university laboratory and get irritated by constant interferences. Therefore, sometimes it's best to participate in the activity like a coworker rather than barge in one someone, micromanaging everything he does.

One particular context which truly tests a leader's skills is "Crisis. Crisis is defined as a situation which poses a threat to the key values of an organization and a timely response is necessary to solve it, otherwise the organization could face serious damage. Organizational as well as individualistic stress is a common catalyst to a crisis. There are 3 types of works that need to be performed in order to address a crisis situation:

1. Cognitive work that needs to be done by analysts to diagnose the situation's scope,

2. Operational work that requires knowledge & experience,

3. Political work that needs to be done by the leaders, i.e. making the strategic choices and getting everyone on board

A successful leader is one who can handle a crisis situation with calmness and knows which decisions to make and which to leave for others. For instance, after the attack on the World Trade Center, the Mayor was intelligent not to get involved in the rescue operations himself. Instead, he reassured the public and promoted calm.

However, effective crisis leadership is not just limited to sharing power with others and leaving them alone. A leader must be prepared for a disaster and build a system that can adequately respond to such a situation. Transactional skills are vital for such a system and soft power alone is not enough for calming people down. For instance, the top leadership didn't reviewed the rescue operations or their progress when Hurricane Katrina stuck leaving all powers to the rescue agencies who were ill prepared and couldn't make a sustainable relief effort on their own.

You can relate well-designed systems to well-directed stage plays. A good director encourages an actor to make entrances & exits whenever they feel comfortable. But delegating all the power is never the answer, as told previously. A good leader needs to review and monitor the system at every milestone to make sure it is producing data flow in the correct manner. Otherwise, there is a very high chance of power individuals grabbing all the power, leaving the leader with nothing but a ceremonial post. The biggest example is that of President Bush senior whose National Security Advisor selected a number of secretaries, all of whom had full access to the President, keeping him in the loop from all angles. But under the tenure of Bush Junior, the flow of information was encapsulated by a number of strong personalities who tailored the information. This lead to a number of problems for the President, which is one of the reasons why his tenure wasn't the most liked one! A number of key people from the White House have highlighted this problem and have stated time and again that the US can't fully flex its muscle due to untimely responses to bad news.

The transactional skills required by leaders as managers should in no case be confused with tidiness of a well-run organization. Instead, fluidity in the work place is dependent on a leader's ability to ensure accurate flow of information making the task of making & implementing decisions simpler. Effectiveness is sometimes more important than efficiency. Franklin Roosevelt for instance ran the country in a manner which wasn't the most efficient but it guaranteed him flow of information from multiple sources. Reagan on the other hand delegated most of his powers which proved to do wonders in the beginning but as he made some bad choices selecting his team, disaster loomed over his presidency.

Top level business leaders can't hope to solve all their problems in a tidy manner. Instead they need to respond according to the situation and gain followers by leading by example. A crucial part of success is making sure bad news reaches the top, otherwise sugar coated information would do more harm than good.

Ross Elkins

Chapter 4

Strategies for Leading in Business

To progress in business, you need to possess the eye for identifying a potential opportunity and capitalizing on it. A good leader possesses the skill set to turn the smallest of opportunities into something big that benefits the company. The strategies and skills discussed in this section of the book will help you navigate the unknown and challenge yourself to take high risks and make smart corporate decisions.

The Enneagram in practice

There are several books written on the application of the Enneagram in business settings such as *Bringing out the Best in Yourself at Work* and *What Type of Leader Are You?* By Ginger Lapid-Bogda, PhD. There are also Enneagram assessment tests that you can take and/or have your team members take. One free test can be found at:

www.eclecticenergies.com/enneagram/test.php.

Authors Riso and Hudson are leading authorities in this sector that have spent years accumulating scientifically-proven research and developing it into what they call the Riso-Hudson Enneagram Type Indicator (RHETI). This forced-choice personality test of 144 paired statements is backed by The Enneagram Institute and is designed as a scientifically valid assertion for professional use in business that may be sampled and purchased through The Enneagram Institute's website. They also provide a booklet that goes into great depth describing each of the nine Enneagram personality types.

Developing awareness of the nine personality types of the Enneagram and one's own personality type eventually leads to intimate self-discovery and professional development. This helps enhance your own growth as a leader by knowing yourself and how to better conduct yourself, and knowing those working under you and how to best approach them in the workplace. It also aids in delegating the proper tasks to the appropriate individuals of your team, and assembling the best crack team to take on a particular project while collectively driving toward future successes.

As a prime example, employing a type 8 - also known as the challenger - will provide vision and confidence. They are someone who likes to take charge of certain projects, because they don't want to be controlled. They tend to work in their own way to achieve their goals. Type Eight generally has powerful instincts and strong physical appetites that they indulge without feelings of shame or guilt. They have a strong confidence and believe in everything they do even it is not in appropriate method or way. However, Type Eight is prone to anger. When severely provoked, or when the personality is unbalanced, bouts of anger can turn into rages. This is because of their desire to be an independent and strong self-confidence, whenever someone gives them a negative feedback, they tend to take it as deeply personal. This is something that can lead to chaos, conflict and misunderstanding.

Type 9 - who is The Peacemaker - will assist in bringing people together and listening to their needs. People of this personality type essentially feel a need for peace and harmony. They tend to avoid conflict at all costs, whether it is internal or interpersonal. They dislike arguments and tend to avoid anything that can cause inappropriate outcomes such as conflict between other team members and tend to have high Emotional Intelligence (EQ). Their inability to tolerate conflict sometimes translates into an overall conservative approach to change. The Peacemaker change can provoke unpleasant feelings and disrupt the type nine's desire for comfort. Type Nine also seems incapable of motivating themselves to move into action and bring about effective change. As they tend to avoid any conflicts, they will try to reduce their interaction with someone in order to maintain their relationship and try not to offend others.

A type 1 - who is The Reformer - will focus on maintaining quality control and the ethical standards you have established. Those in type one are perfectionists who want to get everything perfect, show a good responsibility to their work, are fixated on improvement to be made. They will make sure every word is perfect. They will double-check their work. People of this personality type are essentially looking to make things better, as they think nothing is ever quite good enough. This makes them perfectionists who desire to reform and improve; idealists who strive to make order out of the omnipresent chaos. If you have something needed to be improved, give it to them, they will amaze you in return. Type one is often driven and ambitious, and is sometimes workaholics. But whatever their professional involvement, they are definitely active, practical people who get things done. They are natural born organizers, list makers who finish everything on the list, the last one to leave the office, the first one to return, industrious, reliable, honest and dutiful.

Type 2 is the Mentor. The Mentor always makes the excellent Human Resources representative to serve people and anticipate their needs. They are a helper who needs to be needed. Love is their highest ideal. Selflessness is their duty. Giving to others is their reason for being. They like to help and see other people become successful. They give more than receive. Type two people are warm, emotional people who care a great deal about their personal relationships; devote an enormous amount of energy to them, and who expect to be appreciated for their efforts. They like to help others every time they get approached for help.

The achiever - aka type 3 - may head up the promotional and communication skills of the job. Often, people of this personality type need to be validated in order to feel worthy; they pursue success and want to be admired. They want to achieve their goals and become an employee of the month in their company. They are frequently hard working, competitive and are highly focused in the pursuit of their goals. They will put all effort into their tasks and make sure it has to be the best. Type three is socially competent, often extroverted and sometimes charismatic. They know how to present themselves, are self-confident, practical and driven. Type three people have a lot of energy and often seem to embody a kind of zest for life that others find contagious. They are also good networkers who know how to rise through the ranks. You will notice they always get promoted into a higher rank no matter what they are doing.

Type 4 - The Designer - is the individual who can provide product design and intuition to the impact of the product on customers and affiliates. They are an identity seeker, who feels unique and different from other people. They tend to do something that can make them unique, outstanding and different from others. This is what makes them become creative. People of this personality type tend to build their identities around their perception of themselves as being somehow different or unique; they are thus self-consciously individualistic. However, type four is emotionally complex and highly sensitive. They long to be understood and appreciated for their authentic selves, but easily feel misunderstood and unappreciated. Typically, The Designer is aesthetically sensitive and concerned with self-expression and self-revelation. They are the best when it comes to creativity and innovative.

The investigator - Type 5 - would initiate innovation and contribute technical expertise, because they are thinkers who tend to withdraw and observe. They are generally intelligent, well read and thoughtful and they frequently become experts in the areas that capture their interest. Basically, experts from different departments, fields, industries or areas are made up of Type five personalities. They are the one who has onboard knowledge. However, type five is often a bit eccentric, they feel little need to alter their beliefs to accommodate majority opinion, and they refuse to compromise their freedom to think just as they please.

Type 6 - The Troubleshooter - would make a great regulator of feedback and teamwork. People of this personality type essentially feel insecure, as though there is nothing quite steady enough to hold onto. They are someone who is lacking in self-awareness and confidence. Type six people have a kind of fear or anxiety. This always manifests in worrying, and restless imaginings of everything that might go wrong. This tendency makes Type Six gifted at troubleshooting.

Type 7 -The Enthusiast - is who in a team can provide the energy and optimism necessary to keep the team motivated and moving forward. They are a pleasure seeker and planner, in search of distraction. Type seven is principally concerned that their lives be an exciting adventure. Type sevens are future oriented, restless people who are generally convinced that something better is just around the corner. They like to seek for new adventures as well as risks. As an adventurer, they are naturally born quick thinkers who have a great deal of energy and who make lots of plans. They are well prepared and can make a decision faster than everyone else. They tend to be extroverted, multi-talented, and creative and open minded.

As leaders, we must be able to recognize that different people need to be managed differently because depending on the personality type, people will respond to different kinds of stimuli. By using the details of the Enneagram types to one's advantage, a leader can identify a certain personality type's habits and train of thought so that they can approach that person and motivate them more effectively.

The leader who employs these principles will develop an understanding of how to speak other's languages, which are often very diverse, and then it will become easier to deal with conflicts more fairly. Not only that. By speaking another's language, a leader will be able to get their objectives across more clearly and check concepts with their team members more concisely. Each language has their own specific meaning and it may mean slightly different if another languages is combined. Successful international companies with diversified culture background have spent tons of time and money to hire foreign managers who know more than three languages. This kind of manager is difficult to find, it is like finding a needle under the sea.

The Enneagram in effect helps to diversify a leader's perspective so that they understand nine different ways to solve a problem at all times. They can easily classify their employees into different category during task delegation process. They can better reflect the values they set forth to increase job satisfaction and productivity. With training and practice in understanding the Enneagram, a leader can coach their team members to work at their highest capabilities by developing the insights into what motivates them. With Enneagram, it will also ease a leader to figure out what is strength and weaknesses that need to be improved for maximize productivity. This takes the guesswork out of team assembly and saves invaluable time and also money in greasing the wheels for employees to work together synergistically.

Question the status quo

Smart leaders are always challenging notions, roles and the thinking styles of people around them. Strategic leaders challenge the assumptions and expectations set by other people, encouraging diverse opinions and ideas. If you want to be a good leader, do not be afraid to contest people and their ideas.

This requires an open mind, boldness and patience, which we discussed before as being the qualities required in a leader. Strategic leaders take action after careful consideration of all their options, from different viewpoints, and this comes only after challenging the status quo. They always think outside the box, bend the rules to create something odd, which is innovative and creative. I strongly believe some rules should not be applied into your workplace because it can destroy creativeness and innovativeness. It freezes the idea, talented skills and also the productivity of your team members.

This is assuredly one of the top characteristics of successful entrepreneurs. Great leaders must question the set standard. More importantly, they must have the energy to reimagine their own approach to tasks and consistently reinvent themselves to keep an edge ahead of competition. By maintaining this attitude as a leader, you will encourage your workers to do the same so that it becomes a mindset adopted for the entire organization. Creating this imprint at the core of your organization will keep it running autonomously and well into the future. Sometimes it so happens that a person has a selective approach to tackling a problem that makes them predictable, and in the long run, inefficient. This is caused by external factors such as Political, Economic, Technological, and sociocultural of a country. A fresh outlook is very important when dealing with problems, as not all problems are the same or can be solved in the same way. This requires analytical, strategic and creative thinking about your short term and long term goals. You have to figure out how your short term and long term goals are interconnected to each other.

Well-thought out solutions may sometimes prove impractical because insufficient insight is gathered from the people around the one who is providing the solution.

How to induce the ability to challenge?

- Compile a diverse group of people, and ask them about the long-standing assumptions of your business. See what they come up with; integrate them into your future policies. Transfer your knowledge to them so they can learn more to become better in their job.

- Conduct meetings where open dialogue and conflict are encouraged. Microsoft and Dell are two companies noted for their atmosphere of independently-minded people that are encouraged for their dissimilar points of view to help drive innovation forward. The idea is that perpetuating this creative dialogue will free you as the leader to further focus on pushing the applications of your intellect.

- Come up with a rotating position to keep the status quo interesting and create a challenge among the workers. This has been proven to effectively motivate employees to keep from getting bored at their positions and reduce turnover rates. It is a strategy that fits the pace of the business world today which combines company loyalty with job diversification and improvement of workers' understanding of infrastructure, which serves to advance proficiency.

- Consult third parties not involved directly in the decision making or its outcome to get an unbiased and smart perspective on the consequences and nuances of a decision.

Think ahead

Lapses in judgment are often the result of the inability to detect threats or opportunities in business. The market, technology, economic is always evolving and it only takes a moment for something new to be invented, and so are the needs of consumers. It is necessary to be up to date with current trends in order to maximize profit. In order for this to happen, a leader needs to identify opportunities well in advance so he/she can assign duties and come up with a strategy well ahead of time. If you do not have reading the newspaper or online news websites as a habit, you should start to develop it now, spend 30 minutes in a day reading and increase your knowledge.

Cultivate genuine curiosity in your company's practices and policies, as well as that of your competitors and your business industry as a whole. A funny thing happens when you develop curiosity about a particular subject – a kind of magnetic attraction grows where you are able to draw your attention to multiple values of a particular domain and on top of that, you find yourself enjoying the process, which fuels it even more. You will start to learn more and more. One day, you will find out this knowledge become useful in particular subjects especially when making decisions.

In alignment with curiosity of your business environment, continue to work in expanding your knowledge and experience. You will inevitably begin making relevant associations and seeing patterns across supposedly unrelated fields. Broaden yourself, be flexible, and you will be able to identify the opportunities within challenges to turn your company around. You will find out that almost everything you have learnt are interconnecting. For example, if your business nature is focusing on manufacture, and when you learn about a machine that can help you to manufacture something faster yet cheaper in cost, you can purchase the machine and decrease your production cost and lower the selling price to generate more income.

A good leader may be great at dealing with crises, sure. But sometimes they fail to recognize the weak signals both inside and outside the organization. They spend more of their time on crises rather than to spend time on these aspects. It is necessary to diversify in order to meet demands. Cultivate the ability to anticipate. This can be done by taking into account the perspective of the competitors, consumers and the workers alike.

How can you improve the ability to anticipate?

- Evaluate the performance of your rivals; examine the actions they have taken which baffle you and the ones that have paid off.

- Visualize different scenarios vividly, imagine future prospects and try to plan a course of action accordingly.

- Interact with consumers, suppliers and business partners to get some perspective on the challenges they might be facing.

- Make it a point to visit conventions, conferences and events to get an idea of the booming market trends and practices.

- Conduct market surveys and researches. This can be a costly process and if your employees are not trained to do this, it will not give an accurate result. Alternatively, you can outsource this to company that is specialize in conducting surveys and researches to get accurate information and professionally analyzed data.

Improve your ability to interpret

The best leaders are the ones who are able to interpret well. This is something you have to get from experiences of real world challenges. Challenging situations around you will lead to complex situations and complex information. As a good leader, you must be able to interpret the input you have received and seek the right insights. If you are someone who hates graphs and numbers, this can be a difficulty for you. However, in order to overcome this problem, you can improve your mathematical skills or delegate it to someone who has the potential in your team. Instead of reflexively seeing or hearing what you expect, you should synthesize all the input you have. You'll need to recognize patterns, push through ambiguity, and seek new insights.

Strategic thinking, while commonly practiced as an isolated event only a couple times out of the year, should be a skill that is used on a daily basis. Strategic leaders are the focal point for organizational learning. They promote a culture of inquiry, and they search for the lessons in both successful and unsuccessful outcomes. They study failures. This is the number one difference that separates highly effective leaders from the rest. Therefore as a daily practice, it becomes a frame of mind rather than just a slew of methods. This is why it is such a particularly difficult leadership quality to master if it doesn't come naturally, but with practice and endurance this too can set you and your company leagues apart from competitors. A good leader is able to recognize patterns, identify hidden implications, eliminate ambiguity and approach the situation with a sharp analytical outlook. What good are surveys and researches performed on the market, and observations of the consumers if you are unable to interpret the data and act accordingly? A good leader is expected to be able to connect the dots and come up with a strategy. If you are good in interpretation, you will become a good communicator as well. Below are some tips for you to interpret better.

How to interpret better?

- Try to list at least two to three explanations for any ambiguous data that you are supposed to analyze. Create mock templates of this data and share it with uninvolved colleagues. Compare relevance of your explanations with theirs, aiming to derive any further insights from alternative justifications they come up with.

- Ask for perspectives from stakeholders and unbiased parties. Developing a mental library of relevant information in your business will expand your thinking beyond your current position and daily tasks.

- Consider assigning a mentor or hiring a strategic consultant to train under, whether it is for you, fellow managers, or top employees. Find someone who is more intelligent or has more knowledge and experiences.

- Catalogue any missing information and form a conclusive basis for your hypothesis. Do this on a regular basis and set aside time to practice strategic planning by yourself and in meetings with others

- Alternate between zooming in on the details and out, in order to see the big picture.

- Take breaks, clear your head and Meditate for 10 to 15 minutes, focusing on deep breathing. It brings oxygen to the brain, which nourishes your cells and encourages clearer inner vision. Then think again. Do not burn yourself out.

Pace yourself

Among people, data, strategies, mind frame shaping and policies to manage, the demands of leadership can be overwhelming at times. Keeping up with market trends and groundbreaking innovations can leave you feeling swamped or swept away if you are not able to effectively pace yourself. Sooner or later, you will get bored and hate your work if you are working too hard and too much. A good leader is also a leader who can balance his or her life together with work. In a balanced life, they tend to find more motivation and perform better. So, what makes a good leader? A good leader has the ability to limit himself, a self-cultivated discipline that can contribute and maintain a healthily paced lifestyle. They know their values, strengths, limitations and how to manage their stress, emotion and desire to become a winner.

Consider your tactical footing: you always want to be moving if you are going to make any finite headway for your personal and company goals, so you must maintain a light touch that exerts adaptability, quick decision making, fast redirection of focus when necessary and so on. At the same time, your efforts need to be well planned out and effective enough to make an impression that will carry you through for the long-term, along with your whole company and all the people you are managing.

Such circumstances dictate you to be operating at your absolute best so that you may encourage your subordinates to do the same as well. For this, you need to know yourself well. You must know what you are capable of, how far you can push yourself while still remaining effectual and what habits to practice that ensure a mental, emotional and physical well-being. It is like a riding on roller coaster. Sometime you go fast, then slow down and go faster. Like your work, you have to balance your life and work effectively so you have more motivation and energy to move further. Also, it is not only to give yourself a pace, but your employees or team a pace. You will hurt your team if you push them too hard without enough training. They need time and encouragement and a good leader showing them the pace.

How to pace yourself effectively?

- Stay highly organized with a system that works best for you, so that you get the full scope of where you've been, where you currently are, and where you plan on heading at all times. This can take shape in a combination of schedules, color-coded charts, to-do lists, mind maps, task-oriented applications like OneNote and so on.

- To reiterate, because it is often overlooked or ruled out: take breaks! The brain is a processor, and making it run consistently throughout the day will cause it to overheat and run slower. You think you are doing well now? Are you reaching for coffee or an energy drink? Take short breaks – 10 to 15 minutes – throughout the day to refresh your body and your way of thinking.

- Meditate daily, whenever you get the chance. Take a few moments to tune your mind out of tasking long enough to come back into a sense of calm and inner strength. When you can de-stress and reassure yourself of your power with feeling, you can get back to doing the quality work for which you know you are capable.

- Exercise regularly; build a healthy mind and healthy body. Either early in the morning or evening exercises, it is proven that exercises regularly increase your productivity. Many successful leaders have said they exercise every day before they go to work, as it helps them to be proactive throughout the day.

- Eat healthy foods. Yes, healthy foods. Get yourself filled up with vitamins and minerals required by your body to perform your work actively and healthily without any illness.

- Be highly conscious of time management. Fill your day with priorities and activities that are most important to you and synchronize them with your company goals. Consider where you could tighten up lost time and redirect it into one or a few of those valuable activities.

Find common ground

Strong, strategic leaders do not allow scope for huge conflict among parties that are both involved in the same organizational policy. Here, what works best is finding common ground to unite stakeholders with varying agendas and conflicting views. Find a solution that can satisfy your stakeholders and your employees.

Negotiating and influencing people are the foundation to becoming a good leader. A good leader is expected to build trust and have an active outreach. A leader is the only one who work for someone, the Board of directors, and also the only one who has a group of people working for him or her, in the form of employees. So, leadership is not only about how to lead people to achieve their company goals, they have to be a middleman between the board of directors and employees all the time. With the onset of globalization and diversity in workforce, alienation may arise between sectors of the organization. Regular meetings and increased interaction are important when dealing with fellow leaders in order to overcome hurdles.

People want to enjoy their work and connect with their colleagues. Most people have simply not had enough experience in stimulating positive social engagements or just do not know how to go about it inclusively. Office politics influences are too strong. Managers set a strict rule and cause internal communication to get impassable. Then, they find boredom in their work. On the other side, when people enjoy their work, they develop more creative solutions to problems, feel less stressed, and generally become more efficient and productive. Focus on creating an atmosphere that your team members can look forward to everyday.

How to improve your ability to align?

- Avoid complaints of not knowing by communicating early with employees and making them aware of the tasks at hand. Be specific. Outline objectives in many different forms, such as verbal communication, emails, written reports and so on.

- Identify areas of conflicts and resistance and incorporate them into conversations to expose them. Do your best to be straightforward without placing blame. Focus on the importance of clearing the issue itself rather than trying to pin the source of it. Many rumors and office tiffs grow into problematic distractions because they find their power in the background and whispers. Once they are brought to the forefront so that everyone is aware, that power is lost.

- Monitor the positions of stakeholders carefully during the implementation of your strategy.

- Look for coalitions and hidden agendas and then map the positions of external stakeholders on your initiative.

- Reward the workers who offer their support to team alignment. Give them opportunities to lead teams for small venture projects or assist in organizing group events where possible. Divide them into subgroups for more effective and efficient performances. Workers appreciate experiences that allow them to boost their skills.

- Strategically plan team-building exercises on a regular basis to enhance employee cohesiveness. First identify the purpose of the exercise – if your effort is just a good idea without any real planning involved, it can backfire on you – do you want to increase communication between your employees? Boost morale? Establish trust? Then fit an appropriate exercise to your desired purpose.

Neuro Linguistic Programming (NLP)

To review back briefly about the Neuro Linguistic Programming background, Neuro-linguistic programming (NLP) is an approach to communication, personal development, and psychotherapy created by Richard Bandler and John Grinder. The neurological system regulates how our bodies function, language determines how we interface and communicate with other people and our programming determines the kinds of models of the world we create. Neuro-Linguistic Programming describes the fundamental dynamics between mind (neuro) and language (linguistic) and how their interplay affects our body and behavior (programming). It is also believed that this Neuro-Linguistic Programming can treat common psychology problems, allergies and even the common cold. Additionally, it is helpful in virtually every aspect of personal and inter-personal relations in an organization or company.

NLP enables better awareness and control of oneself, better appreciation of the other person's feelings and behavioral style. When we reach it, we will learn about empathy and teamwork. It also can improve our communication skills because Neuro Linguistic Programming offers an overall understanding about one to one communications. NLP is also a tool of improving Emotional Intelligence (EQ), such as stress management, self-confidences and self-awareness. NLP also increase the skills of customer relationship management (CRM), hence increasing sales and reducing customer loss. This is because NLP can help them to set clear goals and define realistic strategies and understand to reduce stress and conflict.

Successful leaders are frequently on the lookout for ways to improve themselves and be more effective in getting things done.

As the working world grows and we extend our outreach into vast global networks, the need to be more impressionable rises. Our ability to speak to others' interests in order to gain closer relationships demands new skill sets that help to refine our approach.

As people learn more about each other, indeed, as we learn more about ourselves and how our brains operate, we begin to delve into the subtleties that cause a greater impact and bring about more significant change in how we see the world and what we are capable of doing within it. The most important aspect of this change as we evolve is to see it as a behavioral shift rather than an intellectual skill to be acquired.

How to encourage easier, faster connections?

- Look into programs that offer NLP training workshops for businesses that you and your teammates may attend. Research the benefits and make a proposal to your superiors to get company funding for the event.

- Understand that everyone's successes and failures are based upon the way we see the world. Our perceptions define our reality. This is why the core principle of so many motivational seminars is to think positively and make those positive thoughts as much of a reality with daily affirmations and vision boards as possible until they actually manifest.

- Respect others' viewpoints. The sooner you understand that we all think differently, the faster and more capable you will become in communicating with others on a higher level of quality. You will eliminate assumptions of what others mean by developing a keener interpretation of multiple viewpoints.

- By all means, be adaptable. Trying the same thing and expecting a different result is a good way to turn Einstein in his grave. Flexibility opens doors to stronger relationships and increased influence. It also lubricates the learning process by taking a different approach to previous mistakes and alters the thought patterns that keep us repeating the same results, like, 'People don't understand what we're trying to do here.'

Make efficient decisions

In times of turmoil and uncertainty, it falls on the shoulders of those in authoritative positions to make the tough calls and make decisions even without sufficient information, and do so fast. Even in such a situation, smart leaders are expected to carefully weigh their options without getting locked into making go/no-go decisions. Leaders are expected to have faith in their convictions and take both short and long-term goals into account even when forced to make a decision quickly.

Try to approach situations in a methodical way; do not limit yourself to yes/no proposition. It is crucial for a leader to say "No" to something he or she is not interested in. A good leader doesn't let him or herself get cornered into making a choice without being offered the alternative to come up with their own solution.

How to improve your ability to decide?

- Include your team in the decision-making process. Ask them about other possible options. Take it as references but make your decision based on your long-term goals. Their ideas are great but they may not think in long term to achieve your company goals.

- Split big decisions into smaller components and aim to understand unintended repercussions better. Handle the important decision first. If you have someone who has potential, delegate it to him or her.

- Evaluate the team you want to be directly involved with the decision making, based on how you think they may influence the success of your decision. This is another area where implementing the use of the Enneagram would be highly effective. Considering the nature of the problem and the specific topics involved, you can determine which personality types would be best suited to handle the situation.

- Experiment, instead of playing big bets in haste. The best counteraction for unexpected circumstances or foreign territory is to be prepared. It sounds contradictory – how can one be prepared for something unexpected? Look to business forecasts. Stick to your team's core strengths. Allow experimental side projects for your most efficient team members before surprises occur to fan out your options for when they do.

However, some successful leaders found out that decision making process is often a time consuming process especially when you are making decision with a group of people from your company. Everyone who in a meeting room usually comes from different departments such as marketing and sales, product development and design, finance and so on. Because of this, everyone will have their own opinion about something, they have their own standpoint, but after hours spent in the meeting room, they get nothing but awkward arguments. So, from their years or decades of decision making experiences, they recommend other leaders should only invite a few people at the same time, which also means group by group. It hastens the decision making and people tend to voice more opinions within a smaller group of people in order to avoid any inappropriate consequences.

Less can be more, take the best. "Take the best" means that you reason and calculate only as much as you absolutely have to; then you stop and do something else. For example, to explain this in more detail, imagine if there are 10 pieces of information provided by your employees placed on your workstation. They are pieces of information that you have to weigh into a thorough decision, but one piece of information is clearly more important than the other. Many successful leaders believe that less can be more and that one piece of information is often enough to make a decision. You don't need the rest; other information is just complicated reports and they would be wasting time to read and analyze them.

Other than that, successful leaders also believe that if you want to effectively make your decision, you should know clearly what your objectives are and your long term goals before and during the decision making process. If you forget about your objectives and goals, you will get lost and get frustrated. As mentioned before, you as a leader, should make your decision most of the time to show your authority and then implement your decision together with your team.

Ross Elkins

Chapter 5
Business Coaching

"Give a man a fish, feed home for a day. Teach a man to fish, feed for a lifetime" – *Confucius, Chinese philosopher.*

Leadership is not just about influencing people and negotiating with them; leadership involves building a task force that is motivated and skilled enough to tackle the work at hand. The ability to coach has made its way to one of the added qualities of a good leader. Nowadays, workplaces operate on the belief that the workers need to develop simultaneously. Few managers can make it as far as being able to perform coaching work. Coaching aims at helping people learn how to grow, rather than giving directions. They believe if you give what you have to your employees, they will pay you back in a way that will benefit you and also your company.

While coaching their subordinates, leaders must keep in mind the following aims:

Building trust

Coaches must have a lot of patience, establish boundaries and invoke trust in their subordinates and fellow workers. The hardest part is when you are coaching someone who is a slow learner, especially among the senior employees. It can tackle your emotion in the matter if you have a fair amount of Emotional Intelligence (EI).

The concept of trust in the workplace is somewhat of a tricky one. It may appear straightforward and simple to some, but it should not be taken for granted. It may seem to be too much effort to be worth the time or simply frivolous for others, although the effects of established trust among employees in the workplace has proven to provide boundless prestige for the company as a whole.

Way back when business and industry first found their footholds within society and began developing legitimate, long-standing reputations, up until about the mid-90s, organizations felt they had the upper hand when it came to maintaining employee loyalty. Often times that was simply the way it was – employees would compete for jobs within a company and spend the rest of their working life in the hope of climbing up the ladder and earning a pension upon retirement. Their success and job security was dependent upon remaining loyal to their company, whether they agreed with the company's values or not. Transferring from one company to another in those days often meant either starting in a lower position or working to earn their superiors' trust all over again for years on end.

The game has changed quite a bit since then, right around the turn of the century. Now it is the companies competing for employee loyalty for many reasons. Companies face a frequent consideration to either hire new managers from outside the company or promote from within. Employees have a greater flexibility to choose in honing their skills with one organization or packing up shop and moving to another that will better suit their needs, whether that may mean a greater potential for promotion, better pay, more lucrative perks, or a friendlier company culture.

Now the responsibility of establishing trust within a company falls on the leaders and coaches within the various levels of that company's infrastructure. Leaders are called to become excellent representatives of their organization's values and mission as well as that of their specific branch, themselves as their own word, promises and actions, and the affiliates under their direction. Therefore, they have to be the best one in their company to show as guidance, as "monkey see monkey do." They must take it upon themselves to make sure that everyone in their guidance system is working cooperatively and is focused as a whole toward the bigger picture. And the way they may succinctly achieve that is by building trust in the workplace, beginning individually.

If you are doing business in South East Asia countries such as Singapore, Malaysia, Thailand, Indonesia, Vietnam and the Philippines, it is crucial for you to build trust with your employees. This is because of their cultural belief in "GuanXi" which is also known as relationships. "GuanXi" is very necessary to them in their daily life. If you have a good GuanXi with your client or employees, you will be amazed by the outcome when you need something to be done. GuanXi helps you to build a deep relationship and a trustworthy one that can only can be found in Asians. Once they start to trust you in GuanXi, they will give everything they can to you. They will put their effort into the work, they will not ask any questions when you ask them to do something and will be totally loyal.

The key components to building trust with your employees has actually already been outlined throughout this book, so they will be outlined here again and if you should need a more in-depth refresher, you can refer back to these specific sections.

What does it take to build trust?

Good communication skills – Be precise and to the point, explicitly outline your expectations and cover any ambiguous areas. Check for understanding among your employees with questions that elicit specific, detailed responses. Make sure your message is delivered and expressed clearly. Talk to them in a polite way but with the authority of your position. Also, remember your non-verbal communication, hand gestures, body language, facial expression and standing or sitting style when you are communicating with your employees. When you are communicating with someone, remember; do not cut off their words. Let them finish what they are saying. By then, they will feel you have shown your respect that they expect and, in return, they will respect and slowly this kind of behavior builds up trust.

Sometimes, you can add in some humor into your conversation, as it will also decrease the barrier between you and your employees. When you are asking question, ask open-ended questions, and let the audiences think in more detail and be willing to share more.

Good listening skills – Look deeper into your employees' verbal expressions for what they really mean and what they are not saying as well. To get rid of distraction, you should turn off your monitor screen, and turn your mobile phone into silent mode. Look into their eyes when listening to them as this increase your attention as well. Look for words that describe feelings. Develop a keen sense of what their facial expressions and body language is telling you that their words are not, and then acknowledge it aloud with them. Always be aware of their emotional and nonverbal communication languages. Meanwhile, try to smile slightly when listening. Repeat back what they share with you to show your understanding and correct any misinterpretations. You also should reply to all questions asked with truthful answers.

Being open – Employees will have a difficult time trusting you if they can't even reach you. Make sure you have free time for employees to reach you. For example, you can have a day without any meetings to put aside for a discussion with your team. Be prepared to disclose your own feelings and beliefs to encourage others to do the same. Make your employees aware that you are available to them. Practice patience with them instead of being short. Your work priorities are important, of course. However, the employees you manage collectively make a greater contribution to the company, and in a leadership positions and their performance is ultimately your number one priority. You should also encourage the speaker to elaborate and to define their problems.

Being consistent – The more consistent you are in your actions, your words, and following through with your promises through good times and hard times, the more you convey to your subordinates that you are reliable. When they know for themselves that you are reliable, they will be more apt to place their trust in you. Trust is created by earning it with the right actions, thinking and decision making. Keep in mind people will forgive many things where trust exists, but will rarely forgive anything where trust is absent.

Motivate! – Motivation is like food for the soul. The person who is able to effectively arouse inspiration within another person will be remembered and respected for a long time. This is an invaluable asset for you to develop as a leader, so get to know your employees and what drives them, and then find creative ways to stimulate that drive and provide opportunities for your employees to exercise it.

Motivation can be built up in two ways, Intrinsic and Extrinsic motivation.

Intrinsic motivation is motivation that is stimulated from within one's self. One of the best ways to motivate is to tell a story either from real life or one used to convey a message. Most people can come up with several traumatic stories from their pasts where they have given or received negative feedback. Tell them how to convert it into a positive feedback and use it to grow stronger and better. People tend to remember stories easier than theories. You need to motivate them so they feel curious, honored, and feel they have status in the company. Let them feel they are important and that without them, your team is not able to perform specific task.

Extrinsic motivation means the motivation that is stimuli from outside sources. It is usually something that is tangible and gives something rewarding for the individual performing the task. Most companies use monetary means to reward their employees. These including Employee of the Month awards, ranking rewards and commission rewards. You can find those in financial sector and Insurance sectors. The workers in these two sectors are high achievers who break the expectation in monthly sales and competition drives their motivation too. Competition shapes up better employees but if it is too strong, it could drive them crazy and decrease their productivity. So, be careful how you use it. One brief caution when dealing with trust in the workplace is that you do not want your employees to come running to you every time they have a problem or be divulging information that is too personal or practice conduct that goes beyond professional boundaries. This will not only cause a bad reputation for you, but also degrade your company reputation. It is a common phenomenon known as transference that when people recognize a person as powerful and place their trust in them, they may lose their sense of what is appropriate in the professional relationship. Be firm in establishing boundaries. Practice your assertiveness to your employees by letting them know that while you are open and available to them, you are in a professional workplace and your relationship must remain on this basis. It will also increase your employees' productivity as they learn how to solve a problem by themselves.

Provide assessment

Regular feedback lets people be in the know-how regarding their performance, and provides them with self-awareness. Giving feedback often easily offends the receiver, so it is important for you to give honest feedback but in appropriate language and style. To create useful feedback, it must be consistent as well. Clearly, performers can only adjust their performance successfully if the information fed back to them is stable, accurate and trustworthy. Tell what you have observed, why it is important to them and how they should react to the feedback to make improvement. It needs your communication skills to be well developed to give good feedback.

You'll want to make sure that every assessment you make of your employees is geared toward their improvement. So then, do you think that blunt criticism is going to make a productive imprint on an employee's performance? Perhaps, actually, it just might. As a coach of many different kinds of people, you cannot apply a one-size-fits-all approach to every person. Some managers do this, and while they may achieve some results, they are meager at best. Your goal should be to optimize each of your employees' potential. In order to do that, you must treat them as individuals and understand which style of appraisal they best respond to. Understanding the psychology of the Enneagram can help you do this. It allows time for the reviewer to ask more questions or to get better clarification. Along with the appropriate time, make sure to give effective feedback in the appropriate conditions. This also depends on whether or not the feedback is individual group based, etc.

For those who are direct, no-nonsense types of people that like to work hard, blunt criticism may just be the appropriate thing to spur them on. The fact is that you can address these people in a straightforward manner for the most part because you will be speaking their language, and they will appreciate that. Give them the feedback that is clearly explained and focus on key points only. Avoid unnecessary comment or feedback. On the other hand, for those types of people who are more sensitive or are constantly seeking approval for their work, a sympathetic and thoughtful approach in turn will help get your message across more resolutely. You need to take an active role in getting a feel for how each of your employees respond best. Remember to pause and ask for the other person's reaction. This is to give them time to think through what you've said and react to it.

For longer term reviews you can practice techniques like the compliment sandwich. This involves highlighting positive qualities of your worker's performance at both the beginning and end of the assessment. It provides encouragement and a buffer for serious adjustments or improvements that need to be made, which you can address in the middle of your review. The worker will walk away with a level perspective of their strong and weak points, and they will be more confident in rectifying those areas that they need to work on. Remember that like anything that needs maintenance and supervision, your workers need feedback and monitored in their progress on a regular basis. Waiting until performance reviews at the end of the year will not cover all the small changes that could really help your employees progress week to week. Do not wait until then. Make it a weekly practice, but make sure that the material you submit to your workers is of high quality. If there is nothing in particular that you can think of for them to improve, give praise for specific things they did well or suggest that now is the time they can work on pushing themselves beyond their limits into new territory.

Keep your employees informed of their performance on a regular basis and they will be better able to gauge their progress by themselves over time. You will be instilling an important value of self-assessment that will help add to the scope of the employees' purpose in the company and how their work makes an exact contribution to the company as a whole. This reflects on your leadership.

Another tip is to keep your feedback brief and clear but focused on the key points only, so they can understand clearly. One way of doing this is to have the receiver try to rephrase the feedback received to see if it corresponds to what the sender has in mind. No matter what the intent, feedback is often threatening and thus subject to considerable distortion or misinterpretation.

An assessment or feedback is also has to be ongoing process. It is not only just an assessment or feedback when you receive it as ongoing process, but also having opportunities to apply it. For example, playing computer games or mobile games such as Angry Birds, Flappy Bird and other games is a great source to get feedback and self-evaluation. Games give you the key to substantial improvement and the feedback is both timely and ongoing. You often fail to achieve your objective, but you learn about something and from your mistake. With second chances, you know what caused the mistake and you can apply remedial action immediately. The ability to quickly adapt one's performance is a mark of all great achievers and problem solvers in a wide array of fields. The same goes to every aspect.

However, I have extra tips for giving good feedback and assessment based on my experience. I think it is a brilliant idea to choose and address only one issue or problem at a time! If you address too many at one time, it feels like you are complaining rather than giving feedback. This is what is believed to cause conflict and misunderstanding among leaders and their team member or employees. Many leaders turn their feedback into a fight. Focusing on too many issues or problems at once is confusing and overwhelming. Besides that, do not be too critical or focus too heavily on the negative assessment or feedback. Assessment or feedback should inspire the other person to improve, not make them wallow in where they went wrong. They will feel guilty and demotivated. Giving a piece of good assessment or feedback with negative feedback makes it easier to swallow. At the same time, feedback shouldn't avoid real problems. If there's an issue, don't be afraid to state it.

Support and encourage

Coaches are expected to be good listeners, and allow workers to vent without judging them harshly. Employees are encouraged to reach towards their goals. They support and encourage their team members or employees by giving them feedback and transfer their knowledge and experiences to them. A good leader knows what giving means. We have to give first before receive and if they want their team members or employees to grow stronger, good leaders need to give as much as they get as their company also will grow stronger.

When it comes to good listening skills, it's not just about hearing what others say; it's about hearing what they *don't* say and what they actually *mean*. This can be extremely difficult since we all interpret information differently, even the same information, and we all have a tendency to assume we know what another person is talking about when we are really only seeing it from one point of view – our own. However, to master this skill, non-verbal communication skills become essential that a good leader should learn it in today world. With this skill, they can figure out who is lying and who is telling the truth.

The first step towards being able to support and encourage others is to take your own ego out of the picture. This means adopting an unassuming, open-minded approach toward people to achieve the most desirable outcome. Often times this also means achieving the desired mutual understanding of a conversation by addressing the other person's concerns first before even bringing up the actual issue. And sometimes after taking this different approach, the situation resolves itself without even having to address the issue. A good leader always free up his or her time to understand their employees by socializing with them.

How does one do this? The answer is simple – listening. The practice is only difficult because it requires us to unlearn the way we have been taught to get what we want for the good of the big picture and take a different approach altogether. But we can learn this too. It starts with practicing to slow the mind wandering down and place our full attention on what the person in front of us is saying. Focus on his or her facial expression, speaking tone, body and hand gestures and sitting or standing styles. Actions speak louder than words, when someone is speaking, they are often unable to control their body language well.

We are used to being barraged with information and priorities in and out of the workplace so much that it can become overwhelming for our minds to process. Meditation helps, which is essentially the practice of focusing our attention onto a single point of reality and thereby slow all other extraneous thoughts down. It elicits mental peace and clarity, which are necessary for good listening.

Stop interrupting. It requires practice and patience, but try not to complete another's sentence for them. Do not answer their question by questioning them in return. We often want to share an understanding in what others are saying so readily that we make the mistake of assuming what the other person is thinking when in fact, we are far off the mark. More often than not, we assume incorrectly. It is important that each party can show mutual respect to build better relationship, especially in workplace.

We also have the tendency to get caught up in the choice of language another person uses where a little voice in our head will raise a red flag and judge, "This person's grammar is awful," or, "That word is not at all what I would use to describe that." Perhaps the word you would use could describe the situation in another way, but both meanings would still be relevant. Turn off the voice in your head and allow the other person to complete their train of thought so you get the best possible picture of what they are trying to relate. This is essential if you are working with a diversified cultural background company. Your spoken words may have a different meaning to their native languages. Your speaking tone when pronouncing a word also can influence a lot.

The most successful people are those who are able to relate in some way to the people around them. If you make an effort to understand why another person feels the way he or she does, you will gain the referent power based on trustworthiness that Nicole

Lipkin ascribes. The person will feel that they have been heard, and they will be more willing to comply with your instructions. They are likely to have built the trust and confidence in you. Pay attention to subtleties of words that express feelings or needs and body language as well to gain a deeper understanding of how a person actually feels.

Paraphrase what you've heard back to the person to check for accuracy and understanding. Expand upon what you heard the person share from both verbal and nonverbal cues, including emotions, and acknowledge this aloud to the person to confirm your understanding. Do your best not to be critical; judgments are only steps backwards and lose ground with those you are trying to engage. Be honest with how you feel yourself and tell the person what you think after acknowledging what they've said.

Listening requires a great deal of effort, although the rewards pay off big time in the long run because you will have a team full of people who trust in you and understand that their needs and your needs are being met. If you are still confused, read back the previous chapters to learn and practice it.

Challenge their thinking

Coaches are expected to ask open-ended questions, invoke a thinking process for alternative solutions, and motivate risk taking within reasonable bounds.

Open-ended questions are the kinds that go beyond stimulating a simple "yes" or "no" answer. "Yes" and "no," while perhaps answering your question directly, don't really tell you much except that perhaps you should be asking better questions. To get the most information out of your employees, to get a sense of how they personally feel and what specifically can be encouraged or improved, you need to ask the kind of open-ended questions that stimulate discussion. These will provide deeper insights for you and your team and give you all something more pliable with which to work. Alternatively, you can probe to get more detailed answers or feedback. For example, someone says, "I am sad, can I get sick leave?" You should not simply answer "Yes" or "No." You should probe to seek more answers. Ask them why, what, and so on. Let their opinion be expressed and it will let them feel their words are heard by you.

So instead of asking "Were you happy with the results you got?" try, "Why do you think you got results you did?" Most open-ended questions will begin with "What," "How," "Why," or

"Describe to me..." You will find that close-ended questions often make an assumption or implication in their wording that become traps for employees and stifle their genuine thoughts. A few examples are, "Do you think the reports reflect our best productivity?" and "Others are telling me you have been falling short on your quota. Do you agree?" Open-ended questioning should stimulate an employee to think critically as well as generate opportunities for them or the company to move forward positively.

The company Google provides a unique example of how to stimulate their employees' thinking and motivate risk-taking within reasonable bounds. The innovation department of this multibillion-dollar company recognizes passion, one of the four cornerstones of successful leadership, as a bigger motivator than money. Eric Schmidt, a founder of Google, talks about getting people excited about the company's cause. They believe by giving freedom to their employees in their workplace, they can maximize their creativity and productivity. This is why their workplace has living room, bars, sport and fitness center and many more awesome facilities available.

Schmidt believes that young people – students who have recently graduated from college or graduate school – are great examples of people who are ready to be engaged and bring passion into the workplace. There is a reality for us to believe, senior employees tend to be harder to adopt for new changes or methods. You cannot trick an old dog into a new trick. New graduates employees are educated and to use their knowledge and experiences to explore. They learn new things especially technical skills, faster than senior employees. Schmidt wants them to make sure that they take their mission personally. And he and his associates tap into that by allowing engineers to spend 20% of their time working on their own independent projects. Although it doesn't produce golden eggs from a manufacturing standpoint, they claim their method increases experimentation, encourages risk-taking, and allows them to change directions quickly.

Google is also famous (or infamous, depending on who you are) for their unorthodox company environment. Employees can choose to work in their cubicles or take their computers to large, open-spaced corridors in the building rife with large windows and colorful, plush couches. They also make use of cafés located inside the building for a stimulating social environment where they can choose to work or take a break, never too far from the office. They also allow their employees to take a nap in the office or play sport during working hours. They often say that if you want to get the best result from your employees, you have to let them do something in their own way. As you know, Google is a giant technology corporation that has 70 offices in more than 40 countries around the globe. For decision making it tends to be taking longer and is more complicated if it is centralized to headquarters. Therefore, Google used this approach and reached unexpected success. There are also many companies using open culture systems in their workplaces.

Company officials have noticed that by allowing their employees these alternative freedoms, the employees have in turn responded with slews of quality and creative work that have helped keep their company on the frontier's edge. They know their limitations and abilities and balance their work and life perfectly given this environment.

Set meaningful goals

Coaching is redundant if it doesn't have anything to show for it. Coaches are expected to help their employees set realistic goals and help them achieve the same. It is important to set a goal that is common and can benefit in the long term and achieve them by helping each other. As I said before, you have to give first before you receive.

The difference between effective leaders and effective managers is that while both are able to guide those underneath them through the assigned tasks and monitor their progress, successful leaders are the ones who are focused on helping develop future leaders. Managers are more administrative types while leaders are more hands-on, encouraging the successes of their team members to grow into further autonomous employees who develop prosperous skill sets and qualities that may be applied to any relevant jobs and yes, higher positions. Successful leaders are not afraid about their job security, but managers do fear their job is threatened. They hope they can help, lead and share their knowledge with their employees. They want them to grow. Meanwhile, managers are afraid of their job security. They afraid of losing a job and this is why they grow weaker rather than stronger. I have been working for managers or bosses like this and, at the end of the day, I learned nothing but just basic skills, which I could have learned myself.

Rather than do the work for them, however, a leading coach must apply themselves in a delicate balance of involvement that is appropriate to the person's level of capability. Think of teaching a person to ride a bike for the first time – you can support them a number of times, but eventually you have to give them the space to grow and succeed on their own. It is fine to let them fall from the bike sometimes. We tend to remember and learn our lessons once we have experienced it. So, when they go to ride a bike again in future, they will know how to prevent falling. The focus should be on proper initial guidance.

The most commonly used structure for mutual goal setting in the workplace is found in the acronym S-M-A-R-T:

Specific: Well-defined to inform employees exactly what is expected, when, and how much progress toward goal completion. Vague or generalized goals are unhelpful because they don't provide sufficient direction. Once goals are set, explain to your team members why you made the decision.

Measureable: Provide milestones to track progress and motivate employees toward achievement. Set a goal that is based on numeric goals rather than words. For example, your goal is to improve sales. This is an example of bad goal setting. A good goal is set on numeric such as an increase in your sales of 30 percent within the next two months. Also, measure your employees or team members' progress weekly or daily. This means, keep your eyes open and make sure your employees are on the right track.

Attainable: Success needs to be achievable with effort. Make sure that it's possible to achieve the goals you set. If you set a goal that you have no hope of achieving, you are like building a castle in the skies. However, resist the urge to set goals that are too easy for you and your team. By setting achievable and challenging goals, you will raise the bar and grow stronger. A way to know if your goal is realistic is to determine if you have accomplished anything similar in the past or ask yourself what conditions would have to exist to accomplish this goal.

Relevant: It is also known as rewarding. You and your employee should focus on the greatest impact to the overall company strategy. Goals should be relevant to the direction you want your career to take. Make sure the goal you set is in alignment with the mission of your department or your team.

Time-bound: Establish enough time to achieve the goal, but not too much time to undermine performance. There is a specific time frame to achieve this goal. Goals need to come with deadlines, due dates, and payoff schedules. Make sure to set a challenging time frame so you can boost your productivity. Goals without deadlines tend to be overtaken by the day-to-day crises. You may establish a time frame for short and long-term goals. Breaking down any long-term goals into smaller more attainable goals helps to promote achievement and success. Short-term goals are important because they enhance productivity, improvement and motivation for long-term goals.

In order to help an employee set meaningful goals, they must align with the larger goals of the organization. Also, these should be written down goals on board or notes, so they can be referred to frequently. Employees must develop a sense of positional awareness and see how their job fits in with the larger mission of success. In fact, it is common for people who don't understand the purpose of their roles or practice to become disinterested in what they are doing. They are not exposed to it. As a leader, you need to tell them how their work contributed to previous success and what you expected from them.

Consider when you were first learning math applications. There were a bunch of numbers that turned into other numbers, then all of a sudden there were these letters too, and you had to shuffle some from one side of a double-dashed line to the other and it all seemed pretty tedious. The most popular question students ask in math class is, "What is the point?" They see no purpose or immediate application for all of this work they are being asked to do. And then an effective teacher comes along and shares the big secret – the purpose of learning math equations is to train people how to problem solve, to notice patterns and rearrange difficult tasks into more manageable ones. All of a sudden a large portion of students regain motivation.

You must be this effective coach for your employees by helping them understand the bigger scheme of the organization to make those adjustments when they get in a bind. Coaching is a useful way of developing people's skills and abilities, and of boosting performance. It can also help them to deal with issues and challenges before they become major problems. If an employee understands this well, they should be able to describe how the purpose of their efforts add to the larger strategy at all times. You are helping them develop that integral scope.

The Harvard Business Review outlines a great deal in effective goal setting. They suggest holding individual meetings with your employees and asking them to come up with goals that directly contribute to the organization's mission. Individual meetings are less time consuming and always will end with a beneficial outcome. When he or she has offered their initial goals, have a discussion with them to determine if those goals are realistic and challenging enough. You don't want them to bite off more than they can chew, at the same time you want them and they should want to push themselves outside of their comfort zone. You can reflect back with accuracy to show that you're paying full attention and really listening and confirms that you have digested the right information. Always summarize and probe the question for more detail. After the end, you can provide feedback for your employees to develop their skills.

This should be a corroborative effort between you and the employee. It is important to listen to them and their own sense of capability, because while you want the best out of them, they will come to resent you and perform poorly if you push them into goals that are too challenging to accomplish. Likewise if you do not push them enough, they will not grow and your company as a whole may start to lag. Lag - it sounds fine in short term goals, but in long term, you will face a lot of problems especially internal organization problems. You will eventually find that your company growth is slower and slower. Then, to overcome or handle it, you have to waste a lot of time and money to tighten the gap. Therefore, start building your goals together, start now. Time is precious. Find the balance of these 'stretch goals' for each employee and you will notice an increase in the momentum of the organization as a whole.

The next step after establishing goals is to ask your employee how he or she plans to meet that goal. This objective should be largely handled by the employee himself to encourage that sense of strength and self-reliance. Remember that you are acting as a guide. If you give guidance too often, your employees' performance will fall as well. This is because your team depend on your too much and whenever they need help, they will seek your help. Have them break the goals down into individual tasks and set mini in-between objectives to be reached. Many leaders and their team members or employees think that from the beginning the goal is just an exercise to convey the appearance of progress, but there's no hope of achieving it. They did not take it as part of goal achievement process. Concept-check with them to see what they feel the proper landmarks may be. Ask them to consider what risks and challenges they may encounter along the way and how they plan to deal with them. An added consideration is to incorporate what people the employee may be dependent upon to achieve their goals so they train themselves to keep looking at the larger picture. Problem solve with them on how they may best influence those people to see the objectives through to completion.

While you want to encourage your employees in this process to be able to fend for themselves, you must also maintain that balance of assuring them that they are part of a unit, and their goals are your goals as well as the company's goals. Motivate and inspire them, tell them you need their contribution to achieve shared goals. Monitor their progress regularly – before they hit their proposed landmarks – and you will help nip any problems in the bud early on. Check in with them on a weekly basis and since each employee performs differently, be sure to ask them what level of monitoring and feedback would be most helpful. This can be done through the individual meetings, a fast, efficient and effective way to obtain direct feedback, as they tend to talk more in private. Remember that everyone needs continuous feedback and coaching, and the more succinctly you can provide this for them, the tighter your ship will be running. Once you have free time, talk, motivate, inspire and share your knowledge with your team members or employees.

You want to be building relationships with your employees throughout this process but not the friendship kind of relationships. The more comfortable they are with coming to you when they incur an obstacle, which commonly happens when striving to reach objectives, the better you will be able to help them solve problems immediately or rework a goal that needs tweaking without backtracking too much.

Remember that your employees are people too and have personal lives, so take into consideration what their personal goals are in the context of work. To help employees have a sense of purpose in a company and feel motivated, it is important for each one of them to have personal and shared goals. It is common for employees to establish personal goals during an annual review, but the creation and review of ongoing and new goals can help increase an employee's success. You will effectively get more out of the person, because you are addressing them as a whole instead of just a part of work. Be open and ask them if they have any personal goals that they would like to share with you. They should do this only if they feel comfortable – it is their chance to take a step forward, so if they don't take the initiative when you open the door to them, don't push them into it. You can always provide other opportunities for them later.

Then ask how you and the company may adapt to help them reach these goals. This puts a sense of control in the hands of the employee to own up to their goals. Make sure that his or her personal goals align in some way to benefit the team, branch or company as a whole also, otherwise it will become a distraction for everyone. If not, you can provide training for them.

Sometimes the inevitable happens after all precautions are taken into account and goals still can't be met. It will be your job to find out why and hold the people involved responsible for it. This may include yourself as the coach. Whether the employee was within control of the failure or was not, or you had contributed to the problem in some way, you must find out how to rectify the situation or make sure that it can be avoided in the future. If the problem was in the employee's control, have them review the proposed solutions that you two had worked out together during their goal setting and have them try it again. If it was out of their hands or they were too bold in making that goal, acknowledge it but don't dwell on it. Make sure that you both learn from it for future reference. You also can share your experience if you made the same mistake before. Tell them the story and how you learnt it and view this as an opportunity to improve and grow.

If in fact you had made a contribution to the error, be bold enough to put yourself under the scope – were you a bit too neglectful in the monitoring process? Did you not provide enough or specific enough feedback? You must not shirk away from taking responsibility where it's due. If you happen to be at fault and admit it, your employees will respect you more for it by cultivating a well-rounded understanding in the workplace. It is one of the methods to motivate and inspire your team members or employees. Have an open discussion about what differences you will make for next time; do it through promises and take action based on it.

The integration of coaches makes for role models in the workspace that build better relationships between workers and achieves higher goals.

Chapter 6
Leadership & Management

For the past couple of years, it has become a fashionable trend to distinguish sharply between leadership & management however, with the passage of time and in light of recent evidence, it is being found that the distinction may in fact be misleading.

The contrast between leadership and management began all the way in the 70s when a leader was presented as an artist who uses his innovativeness and creativity to drive the company out of chaos. On the other hand, a manager was seen as a person who uses his problem-solving abilities to keep the company within control. Since then, the gap between leadership and management has widened and now approached to such an extent that many companies place completely separate requirements when hiring leaders & managers. A leader was defined as a person whose only job was to put forward a vision and strategy while a manager was defined as a technician who has the tools to get the job done. The distinction is much like an engineer and a scientist where a scientist puts forward a theory while an engineer applies it in the practical world.

However, central to all these differences is the orientation towards change. This particular concept was highlighted by John Kotter whose work in 1990 concluded that management is all about coping with the complexity of a job while leadership is about coping with change. He stated that good management is necessary to maintain calmness & order in an organization whereas leadership is required to keep the organization dynamic and on wheels.

Here's a table that will show you the well-established difference between a leader and a manager.

	Leadership functions	Management functions
Creating an agenda	A leader's job is to establish a clear direction about the company. He needs to have a vision for the future and should develop strategies that will lead to that vision getting achieved.	A manager on the other hand has to deal with the technical side of things like budgeting. He has to decide the best course of action that would be the most sustainable and affordable, keeping in mind the company's finances.
Developing people	Aligning people; a leader has to communicate his vision and sell it to his employees so they would put as much motivation as possible to get the work done.	Organizing & staffing; managers have to decide on the staff that will be most usable for implementing each strategy forwarded by the leadership.
Execution	Motivating & inspiring. Leadership needs to energize the people in the workplace and believe in them so that they don't get stuck somewhere or worse get disappointed.	Controlling problem solving. A manager must actively monitor how employees are performing and reorganize the structure if he thinks the system is bogging down.
Outcomes	Leaders sometimes produce positive & dramatic changes after their plans have been implemented.	A manager on other hand promotes consistency and predictability.

Ross Elkins

By now, you must be viewing management as an inflexible bureaucratic type of job which requires a person to do the same things over and over again. However, even John Kotter agreed that in the end a leader cannot survive without being a good manager. Leadership may be different from management but it's not because one involves lesser paperwork than the other. Leadership isn't something full of mysticism. And it's definitely not born within a person. In fact, leadership is something that a person develops within himself as he is given charge of a situation. In order to become a great leader, an individual must be aware of the ins and outs of the entire organization and can't simply rely on his gut and motivational speeches to get the job done every time.

Despite the popular literary appeal of separating the two, many researchers and corporate bosses still doubt whether they are really as separable as they are portrayed. There is a considerable amount of resistance on the way that management is shown as something boring, uninspiring and expendable. Many people have publicly opposed such ideas and have stated that the "down with the management and up with the leadership" approach won't bring out anything good. As a leader has the upper hand and he is the one who decides what kind of manager he want, he should try his best to bridge the gap and bring a sense of continuity, especially during times of change. He must be aware of the majority, if not all of the processes of the company and must actively contribute within the development of newer practical implementations rather than sitting back and forwarding his vision to the manager. At the same time, he shouldn't micromanage; a simple suggestion would be better than an order.

Much research in recent times has shown that instead of being separate entities, leadership & management are essentially part of the same job, split into two. It has been found that leadership is one of the traits that every manager must possess in order to keep running the business in a successful manner. Much of the complexity and confusion arises from differentiating the two which sometimes leaves a lot of no-man's land in between. We often talk of managers and leaders as people who are incompatible with each other. Leaders are considered as charismatic, dynamic people with inspiring personalities where managers are seen as boring people with a pile of paperwork on their desks.

However, such a view doesn't coincide with the reality on ground. A manager for instance is recruited to take care of a variety of tasks in a dynamic manner like planning, implementation and even strategic thinking. These tasks aren't done in a corner office but instead are carried out after taking every employee's feedback. In addition, inspiration & motivation have been found as key traits that a manager must possess in order to keep the company running smoothly. Interestingly, you would notice that the same is expected from a leader. Therefore, in the end the 2 are essentially the same thing.

This does not mean that every company should merge the job into one. Instead this means that managers should be promoted as leaders while leaders should know the workings of their managers. Only then can a company survive. In conclusion, the contrast between managers and leaders can be harmful for the company and as a world as whole in the long term. More people are focused towards becoming leaders rather than managers because they see them as something boring people do. A leader should consider the advice of his manager on important "visionary" and "strategic" matters and should keep in touch with the day to day activities of the company so that he is well connected with the people on the ground.

Chapter 7
Retaining your Employee

Employees are basically the driving force that ensure that an organization runs smoothly and develops in line with the leader's vision. If the employees aren't satisfied with their work then the whole organization runs into the risk of bogging down and eventually breaking down. Employee retention & engagement are critical when it comes to the profitability & growth of an organization. These two factors kick in very early, right at the recruitment stage and the entire process is a never ending one which should be dealt with care & seriousness by the leader.

A famous industrialist, Andrew Carnegie once said that he didn't care about his factories, his railroads, his transportation assets or his money; all he cared about was his employees and if anyone were to strip him of all his properties but leave his employees behind, he could rebuild the entire business from the ground up within 3 – 4 years. The statement was given all the way back in the 19th century and even though much has changed since then, the core principle is still true and holds perfectly. Even in today's information driven & highly competitive world, retaining key employees is extremely necessary for a business to thrive and be profitable for its stake holders. A recent study that targeted over 7500 employees, carried out in 2005 found out the different factors which employees valued the most when they thought of staying with the company.

- 48.4 percent exciting work,

- 42.6 percent career growth,

- 41.8 percent relationships,

- 31.8 percent fair salary,

- 25.1 percent great boss

If a leader pays attention to this statistics then he/she'll conclude that an excellent retention mechanism can ensure employees staying in for the long-term and thus, ensuring maximum productivity. Employers therefore, shouldn't ignore any such policy that will help them increase retention and gain their employees' trust & loyalty. But at the same time they should not put too much focus on this and make sure that their own vision gets ample attention.

In the 21st century, employees often choose organizations/companies that provide them with continuous benefits to keep them from leaving. In return they will show extra-ordinary dedication & impart as much knowledge as possible as a token of gratitude. However, employees cannot keep putting in their sweat & blood into the company if they aren't satisfied or are provided with low grade opportunities for growth. Money is also a significant factor and sometimes is the most important factor that employees consider when thinking about leaving the company. I'll be discussing each one of these step by step. Most employees usually stay with the company if they keep receiving a steady bonus after a certain amount of time but there are some employees who value growth more than money and become dissatisfied with constant raises, prompting them to leave. BridgeGate LLC conducted a study in the year 2000 targeting 600 American workers, asking them what they would want from their employer to keep them from leaving. The results showed that 50.5 percent went for non-monetary rewards which meant that some people are indeed not lured in by a ton of money. The details of the non-monetary factors are as follows:

- Improved benefits program, 23 percent,

- Work schedules, 14 percent,

- Stock options, 9 percent,

- Better training, 5 percent,

The biggest factor that played a significant impact on employees' retention and was inferred from the result was "culture". Employees greatly valued the workplace culture and wanted to be an active part of the company rather than sitting in a corner office day in, day out. It is important for the leader to make the employees feel that they are part of a team and connect them to his/her vision.

There are 2 basic strategies that are interrelated when it comes to understanding employee retention. The first one involves focusing on reasons as to why employees voluntarily leave companies/organizations. Research has found that there are a multitude of pathways that lead to quitting. The second strategy involves focusing on why people stay in a company. Top tier leadership has been drastically trying to solve the enigma of employee retention so that they can render better output. A study revealed that almost 84 percent of employees of the staffing group, Manpower were searching for a new job. The problem is not just finding new employees and training them, but it's also that when employees leave a company they take trade-secrets with them which can kick-off inside trading campaigns.

Employers can raise their level of employee retention by introducing a number of practical strategies that target their workforce. An effective retention scheme would be one that follows multiple routes to employee retention. In the UK, only 10 percent of the people who left the company cited "low pay" as a reason for leaving the job. But you should also know that even though a "high salary" isn't important, a "fair salary" is still necessary if you want to rule out this factor when it comes to employee retention. It was also found that pay raise was not as important as actually knowing what leads to a pay raise! The pay raise curve becomes flat quite soon and employees start focusing on other things like job characteristics, career development, etc.

The factors that can drastically improve employee retention in a company/organization are given below:

Job Characteristics

The term "Job Characteristics" is defined as the degree to which any task/job/work provides sufficient amount of freedom and discretion to the employee to schedule his own work and determine the pathways through which he would want it done. This factor is based on the simple assumption that people not only work for the money but also want a degree of satisfaction & control in their work life. According to research, employees not just want to deliver high quality results but also want to take on challenges as part of their job which prove as an obstacle for their thinking pattern, forcing them to evolve. However, leadership often ignores this fact and dumps easy yet repetitive tasks on its employees which decrease productivity as well as employee retention. It has also been found that if employees' work content is pre-designed in a manner that is suitable for them, i.e. challenging, fresh, etc. then the stability of the work place can be drastically boosted. According to Amabile & Glynn, skilled employees showed much more commitment, interest and loyalty to their jobs compared to non-skilled ones. But at the same time if skilled employees are not utilized in the right manner, then they will eventually get bored and leave the company.

These under-utilized employees end up in a supportive role to the company which is extremely miserable with respect to a skilled employee. Some organizations are aware of these conditions and take active steps to counter them. For instance, some companies keep their employees hungry for more by providing them chances to be creative and pursue tasks that interest them. Remember, whenever a task requires an employee to use his skills in conjunction then it will bring out more loyalty, even if the task isn't of that much value to the company.

Career Development

Career opportunity & development have been redefined thanks to the marvelous, revamped employee relationship strategies being implemented in workplaces all over the world. Development is now being defined as gaining new skills and implementing various techniques that would benefit both employees as well as organization. Employees greatly benefit from career development opportunities by gaining greater psychological satisfaction from their work as well as obtaining the most out of their job. Furthermore, they find a renewed sense of responsibility for their career. On the other hand, organizations benefit from such strategies by getting more loyal employees who are more skilled & productive. So you see, it's a win-win situation.

To organizations, the availability of employees with respect to skill development is a key attraction. In retrospect, if an organization does not pay heed to its employees' needs as well as desire to grow, then "development" becomes a huge issue that leads to resignation. The European Centre for the Development of Vocational Training has reiterated its statement saying that companies need to actively participate & engage in their employee's career development to attract, filter out and retain the best people. When an organizations starts to recognize and adequately respond to its employees' needs, only then will they get the best out of them. Therefore, investment in career development entities is a necessity to strengthen the bond between an organization and its employees. In addition, career development opportunities can result in enhance employees' skills through training programs.

A number of employees are looking for organizations that don't just require textbook knowledge but actively train their employees to be better suited for the job. Many organization actually train their employees so that they could smoothly integrate within the workplace while many provide optional training opportunities that can lead to better positions and new skills. Many individuals, especially young ones are quite energetic and are looking to eat as much possible. Whenever, such employees receive these opportunities they are grateful to the company and are much more likely to commit for a long time compared to employees who are forced to learn everything on their own through fear of demotion.

Lack of career opportunities is one of the reasons why there is a never ending labor deficit in Asia, particularly China & Japan. Employers over there don't take care of their workers as much compared to Western companies which leads to an employee leaving as soon as he meets the experience qualifications for another better company.

Recognition

Every employee is a human being and thus has a need to be duly recognized for whatever he puts up with or whatever he delivers for the company. The more commandment they get, the more likely they are to commit to the organization. Being recognized for a job well done makes employees feel better about themselves and this is a fact that no one can deny. Even a manager feels happy when he is commended by the CEO, even though he knows this is a well-used tactic.

Therefore, organizations should try to prioritize employee recognition and should not leave this to chance. Leaders should actively try to create a positive, healthy work environment in order to promote innovation in the workplace. Because people who are appreciated will not only be more loyal but will also be more productive which is what most employers go after. Furthermore, leaders would find it much easier to align employees according to their game plan if they keep appreciating them on a regular basis.

In 2011, Accenture conducted a survey in Ireland targeting the level of recognition received by employees when they do some good work. The results stated that almost 63 percent of employees who had no plan for leaving the company were satisfied with the amount of recognition they receive whereas 24 percent of the employees were not satisfied with the amount of commandment they received. You, as a leader should keep these results in mind and should therefore make changes that will lead to lesser favoritism and more credit-where-its-due.

If organizations are to ensure that their employee recognition programs are effective, meaningful as well as genuine then they should consider a number of factors. These are listed below:

- The recognition distributed should be fair,

- It should be as transparent as possible,

- There should be consistency when awarding recognition,

- Organization should also mention the reason as to why they are commending the employee, publicly.

Management

Management is basically a process where individuals or leaders work to achieve their visionary goals in an organizational manner. Managers play a great role when it comes to influencing an employee's dedication to the company and as such, their role should be given due importance. In the previous chapter, you would've seen that even though there is a difference between

Leaders & Managers, sometimes their qualities overlap and therefore, leaders have to learn & invoke their managerial side to tackle a situation.

There are a number of managerial retention practices that can drastically improve employee satisfaction and increase the probability of an employee remaining committed to an organization for a long time. It has been found that these practices have a direct relation with the rate of employee turnover. The factors include:

- Scheduling off-duty employees to work,

- Improving top-tier to lower-tier communication gap,

- Limiting training time,

- Making the pay-rate competitive,

- Making the reward mechanism partly public,

These factors must be embedded within the workplace in such a manner that the employees don't feel imposed. Only then can an organization's leadership achieve world class commitment level.

A research was conducted on the very same issue by Mastery Works Inc. which found that one of the factors that had a huge impact on whether an employee wanted to stay or not was whether the employee developed a trusting relationship with the top-tier leadership as well as the manager if there is any. This means that an organization must place special emphasis when employing its managers as well to ensure that the employees feel well-connected with them. The research also found that when an organization's leadership trusted in their employees' capabilities rather than doubting them at every step, assured challenging work, improved the workplace's quality and provided ample opportunities to learn new skills along the way, only then can it trigger loyalty in them.

In the 21st century, where every office is plagued by corporate scandals, having a manager with honor & integrity has become a necessity rather than an option. Therefore, employers should place special emphasis while hiring them as the future of their organization would depend on it.

Work-Life Balance

24 hours a day are simply not enough to tackle each and every work as well as personal problems. Individuals have to juggle between their issues and end up stressed out only to find out they have to repeat the same routine the next day. Work-life balance has become quite a dominant issue when it comes to the quality of workplace especially for people who have a multitude of

personal responsibilities over their heads like family, friends, travel, etc.

Many organizations actually recognize this problem and actively try to solve them by forming hotlines, software and other programs to make sure that the conflicts don't affect their employees' productivity. Employees are calling for more flexible hours and fair work distribution that wouldn't affect their personal lives. Taking care of such a problem would definitely lead to greater employee satisfaction.

Policies that focus on work-life balance, put forward by the leadership can greatly reduce the impact of work on an employee's personal life; this has an inverse effect on the employee's stress levels while at the same time increases his/her productivity & focus on work. For employers, implementing such policies would directly translate into greater employee loyalty and lower turnover. In addition, it will also attract a bunch of skilled employees who could do wonders for the company and are looking for such policies rather than cold-hard cash.

Greenslopes Private Hospital found that when they invested in improving the employees' work-life balance, they reduced the employee turnover rate by 5.5%. At the same time they saved 23 percent on employee compensation costs. This means that the investment would not only give you loyalty but would also save your money in the long run.

Psychological Factors that Affect Employee Retention

Employers should place special focus on the factors listed above if they want to retain their employees' commitment & loyalty. However, in recent times it has been found that these factors implemented in their raw form aren't enough. In order to make the most out of them, these factors should be implemented in a tailored form, targeting the way employees think and what they need. The practice, which is explained below is known as psychological contract.

Basically, a psychological contract is an undocumented and unsigned set of expectations that naturally exist between the employer and the employee. These expectations might be difficult to comprehend as a whole and can be seen as a collection of diverse ideas held by the employee. When these expectation are broken and the employer falls shorts of his unwritten contract, the employee develops mistrust and disappointment towards the organization. This ultimately leads to decreased motivation for the job which becomes zero with the passage of time and the employee leaves.

Psychological contracts are generally promises that are based on obligations of employers towards their employees. These emerge whenever an employee is given the idea that he/she will receive special concessions and priority if he chooses to work for the company. This gives the employee a feeling of influence and power and whenever this influence is taken away, the whole thing comes down.

However, if an employer hasn't made such unwritten promises at the start, then every employee will value clarity in communication and fairness in recognition.

Most research has showed that the majority of employees at a workplace are rather pessimistic about this psychological contract. For example, 50 percent of MBA graduates in the U.S Management School at Midwestern believe that their employers had broken their contracts within the first 2 years. Another study that surveyed employees during restructuring found out that 25 percent of the respondents felt their psychological contracts had broken.

In conclusion, the main concern of any company should be its capacity to engage, develop and retain its "key" employees. The word "key" is of paramount importance here as not all employees are essential for the company especially those who linger around. Organizations should spend their resources on coming with effective retention strategies and should work actively to improve them. Examples include:

- Designing an employee-value proposition,

- Developing a reward system that integrates compensation,

- Give feedback to employees based on their work on a regular basis,

- Build a cultured workplace that engages employees,

- Refining management skills,

In addition, employers should also focus on their personal relationships with their employees. In fact, all of these factors when combined and implemented in conjunction can bring about the change you're looking for. Otherwise, you'll simply be compensating the lack of one factor with another to keep your employees motivated and focused on their work.

Chapter 8
Leadership & Performance

Quite often than not, the link between leadership & performance is taken for granted but if you look in a little bit of detail a leader needs to have a specific set of skills and needs to actively focus on his performance to make it top notch. This chapter will focus on this link and how a leader can enhance his performance using various techniques.

One of the reasons as to why organizations face a lot of difficulty in reading the impact of leadership on their performance is due to the manner in which a number of factors interact with each other. Traditional management as well as Human Resource Management practices that are closely related to planning, organizing & controlling material & human resources are very well connected with leadership practices like setting direction, gathering people, motivating & inspiring them, etc. In addition, performance is not simply something that comes with the passage of time; it is something that is impacted by various other factors. Many of these factors are intangible and abstract which is why the traditional approach to understanding these factors cannot be taken. Instead, we need to take more multi-dimensional & holistic approach. I will also be considering management & leadership side by side as you'll be noticing that the two have more similarities than differences.

The first thing you need to know is that almost every leadership development program uses an MLD – MLC model whereby Management & Leadership Development will lead to enhanced to Management & Leadership Capability which will result in greater overall performance of the organization. In order to decipher the impact of Management & Leadership on a company's performance, one must first know a whole range of issues related with MLD, MLC and performance. MLD & MLC is something you shouldn't be concerned about. However, what you should be aware of is performance.

What is performance?

When reviewing the impact of leadership & management over an organization's performance, there are number of levels you should consider, the first one being the individual level. After an organization begins its development, it is thought that a specific leader/CEO of the company will improve his effectiveness with each passing day. The improvement may be in the form of increased productivity, technical competence and greater knowledge or may be shown by more subtle measures like communication, self-awareness and long-term strategic planning.

The next level that is likely to be effected by improved performance is the "group" level. This level effects the behavior of subordinates and followers of a leader and may be noticed either by hard numbers or by improved communication, morale and spirit. Improved performance may also lead to decreased turnover rate, more willingness to go overtime and better feedback.

The third level of effect that is associated with improved performance is at an "organizational" level. Improving the effectiveness of any organization is the key driver behind leadership & management growth and the relation can be reversed as well. The performance of an organization is directly dependent upon the performance of its leaders at various positions (heads of different departments), so collectively improvement in performance means greater profit for the organization as a whole. The most likely outcomes of improved organizational performance is hard cash, greater investment, increased stock prices, etc.

One of the other key things that you should consider when reviewing your organization's performance is the time delay after a decision is implemented and increased growth. Next, you'll be looking at the relation between leadership, MLD and performance at different levels which will help you better understand the drivers behinds greater growth.

Link between MLD, Individual Capability & Performance

It is widely accepted that working on Management & Leadership Development will enhance the capability & performance of an individual however the real relation is more complex than thought.

It has been found in various studies that MLD doesn't have the type of effect on an individual's skills & capabilities as one would want. Unless and until MLD starts focusing on people actually taking leadership roles and applying their skills in real time, they can't benefit from any training. A recent review carried out in 2004 found that there are 2 factors that almost always have a positive impact on an individual's performance:

1. The inclusion of opportunities for receiving & discussing feedback,

2. The quality of management processes preceding, supporting and strengthening development activities,

Therefore, companies and stakeholders cannot simply rely on MLD training when it comes to improving their organization's performance. They need to discuss and actively monitor an individual's training and take feedback from him/her in order to rectify his weaknesses and build up his strengths.

Relationship between MLC & Organizational Performance

There are two studies that clearly show the link between MLC & Organizational performance.

One of the studies was carried out on data from 800 Sears outlets in the US which showed that attitude of employees towards their jobs as well as motivation level towards their employers was positively linked to the attitude of customers as well as the turnover rate of the store. The key link between the two was the way the Store Manager (in this case he's also the leader) organized the store and kept every employee's need in check. Another study of 100 stores located in the UK found that employee satisfaction on a particular day was directly related to the sales made on that day. It can be seen that performance and employee attitudes are very well linked and the relation goes both ways. If the store does business on a particular day, the employees are more satiated with their work and are thus happy with the organization.

It has also been found that companies whose employees were satisfied with their leadership focused on 4 management practices, namely strategy, execution, culture and structure. When the top tier leadership focused on these 4 entities, the organization automatically improved its performance which lead to greater employee satisfaction & motivation, setting off a self-sustaining chain reaction.

In addition, management competence is more useful in dynamic organizations or in companies going through changes. Therefore, a leader always needs an extra set of skills at hand whenever making his decisions in tough times as the line between management and leadership becomes very thin at this point.

Relationship between MLD & Organizational Performance

Stakeholders heavily invest in MLD programs due to their effectiveness on an organizational level that helps spring out new leaders.

A study by Lee et al. carried out in 1993 found that British Telecom saved close to 300 million Pounds as a result of extensive management training programs. The training program acutely decreased the number of errors carried out by junior managers as well as loss of resources due to incomplete knowledge about the workings of the company. Another study carried out in 1998 found that over 63 percent of firms who had some kind of MLDs were able to notice as well as highlight the positive effects of such programs. The benefits traced include higher morale, shorter response time, greater flexibility and improved quality of work.

In addition to these studies, there are others that highlight a link between Human Resource Management practices & organizational performance. The Management Firm Becker & Huselid stated that management development and training programs are no longer a want but a need for any company that wishes to survive & thrive in the marketplace. In a study of over

100 UK companies, it was found that 18% variations in productivity & 19% in revenue was linked to the management practices being carried out by the people in charge.

Chapter 9
The Don'ts for Good Leadership

While assuming a leadership position, many can get carried away by the power and self-importance, which leads to a dwindling sense of respect among their subordinates. There a lot of things to keep in mind to be a good leader, and among them are a few don'ts that will pave the way to being a more inspiring leader. Good leadership inspires people to reach their full potential and realize goals, while bad leadership makes people feel like they are being forced to do something under the action of authority.

Egocentric outlook

This involves a heightened sense of superiority, where a leader is convinced that they are the most important in their corporate sphere, and that their subordinates do not matter. As previously discussed, it is important that you recognize the needs of those who work with you, and not disregard their importance to the organization. Remember that without having the employees that you lead, there wouldn't be a company to run. A good leader is one who has followers who want to be led by that leader.

Egocentric leadership is a leadership style in which the leader is only interested in him or herself. Egocentricism operates on the belief that the needs and opinions of oneself are of a higher priority that anyone else's, which is a quite negative approach. Such leaders see no limit to their knowledge and completely take no notice of the others. It demoralizes the subordinates and causes resentment. Their employees may feel they are not heard, can contribute nothing and are demotivated. For example, when you talk to someone, but he or she ignores you, do you feel bad? The same theory applies to your employees.

This attitude of assuming one possesses all the knowledge needed for their job puts an immediate cap on their growth. You think you've learned all you need to know for your position? Okay then, you can go home now, you're done.

Successful leaders operate with a sense of humility and awe that they can always learn more about effectiveness in their job, in approaching their employees and eliciting their best work, and about their particular industry (and other related industries). The leader who acts as though they can do it all the work is unlikely to rise to be a great leader, because they'll be too busy doing everyone else's job. They spend whole working day at their desk without any interaction, communication and leadership. The fact that the nature of businesses is always changing, growing, evolving should speak directly to your own stance on business growth.

Being a leader means being a team player, putting your employees and the company before yourself as stated before. So essentially, without the success of the others around you, there is no success for you. You become the person stuck on the island with no passing ships. You should know that without your employees, your company means nothing. Each one of them built your company, you are the king and they are the warriors who fight in a battlefield.

Egocentrism also fosters the idea that one has control over the lives of others, so that others must obey what they ascribe, or they will have to deal with the consequences. This attitude effectually harms the one exerting it because by hindering the growth of others, they restrict their own growth. What happens is stagnancy from where the constantly changing force of the outside world washes away those who are not willing to change along with it.

Invulnerability

Leaders drunk on power tend to believe that they can get away with anything, owing to their high-ranking position. In this belief, they commit many fallacies, thinking that no harm will befall them because they are too cunning and smooth to actually get caught. This feeling of being invulnerable and untouchable creates a divide between the subordinates and the leader and they are put into an awkward position. So, they start to move at a slower pace and become less productive. Soon, if someone in their team who has much more potential than him, he will be replaced. This is because even though everyone is easily influenced and controlled by an authority figure, they may also become more productive with a more positive leader.

Invulnerability sides on the polar opposite of building trust in the workplace. The immediate effect is a reduction in progress among those directly involved. This could be for a number of reasons, whether because the workers operating under the power-hungry leaders become discouraged, disgruntled, or such in-office disorder ensues that the branch becomes inefficient. Cases of malignant behavior may permeate among the workers, or simply trying to manage them becomes more difficult because they develop a resistance to their autocratic manager.

Being over-friendly

In good leadership, you want to come across as approachable, and that is great. However, bad leaders are known for becoming too friendly with their subordinates, to the extent where the employees start to not take the leader too seriously anymore. Whenever someone makes a mistake, he will forgive them easily and feel bad if they give punishments or lousy feedback. They treat their team as their friends. There is an old saying "Never becomes a close friend with your colleagues." I find it meaningful because it can stop you from becoming a leader who is responsible. You can be nice as long as you are prepared to make difficult choices when they are necessary, like firing the wrong person for the job, and keeping a rational perspective about it (that person would only drive customers away or keep other employees so entangled in their poor habits that it would drive team harmony down).

Micro-managing becomes a problem when your employees are being difficult and you feel bad about telling them that they've committed a mistake and that they need to rectify it at any cost, especially when they are your friends instead of mere employees. This becomes commonplace with the belief or *hope* that the issue will resolve itself over time. Throughout many circumstances that have gone just this way, time and time again they've proven that they need intervention. It's best just to confront the problem from the moment you realize it rather than putting it off.

Bad leaders let their subordinates undermine their authority. They made no choices and decisions. They allow stakeholders to take advantage of their time schedule. They give benefit to customers who are loud and abrasive, demanding free compensation when the company policy statement clearly has them covered. Consider this – if a nice leader continually gives the benefit to irresponsible, ineffective employees, the more skillful members of that group who work hard and see this will grow bitter. Is it fair that the more apathetic employees get break after break while everyone else is following the rules? Eventually the better-performing workers will take their own initiative and leave the company. Then you will be stuck with slacker employees that drive your productivity down and ruin your reputation as a business professional. That is not the kind of leader you want to become.

Be direct and concise with your rules and expectations in the workplace and administer them consistently to prevent this scenario from happening. It may not feel good at first to be 'the enforcer,' but it will over time when you team's productivity shows something for it. Remember that being liked is not the same as being respected. Respect comes with getting results, exerting prowess, and holding yourself and others up to an agreeable standard that boosts morale. Respect will last forever but like can become dislike over a period of time.

You should set a limit and barrier for interacting with your team members or employees. You can set time limit for each informal communication. Keep in mind that you are a leader and that you need to prove your ability to achieve. You should not let something that is not really important to turn into an obstacle and barrier that keeps you apart from your vision.

Failing to provide a pleasant work environment

Being a leader entails managing people and keeping them in check, which may earn you the title of a tough cookie to crack. However, productivity increases by a great margin when people actually enjoy the work that they are assigned and have fun in the workplace. It is up to the leader to provide for an easy-going work environment where people can function to the best of their ability. The workspace should be a comfortable space, where people do not find it difficult to communicate among themselves for the better of the company.

Studies in psychology and architecture have come to understand that a person's physical environment has a direct impact on their subconscious and well-being, linked to how well they will perform. Small confining spaces, sharp corners and dull colors are all anti-motivators that mentally drain a person of their energy and wane inspiration over time. How can a person be expected to become creative and innovative on a regular basis at work when they are surrounded by inadequate stimuli? You should hire a professional architect or interior designer to design your working place, starting from the entrance door to your office all the way to the washroom.

If you have established or built your company building a long time ago, you may not have the chance to redesign the building structure of your organization. However, investing in ergonomic furniture – the kind to effectively accommodate the human body – and arranging internal spaces to be more open and allow for more movement are a few ways you can improve the physical work environment. This means going beyond hanging up the sporadic motivational poster. Buy a quality chair and working desk. Your employees' performance can be influenced by the comfort of the environment in which they work. For example, if the chair is too high or their working desk is too low, it can cause their back to suffer injuries over the long term.

A pleasant work environment includes the overall mood of the workplace too, and largely derives its source of that mood from the leader. Look at what drives you and what pleases you. Treat your employees as you would honestly like to be treated yourself. Bring a high-energy attitude into the workplace because you enjoy being there, and if you don't, take the initiative to make it a place that you do enjoy working in. Nowadays, many companies, even small startups, start to build facilities and infrastructure in their company offices. They build a fitness center, sport facilities and places to relax. They strongly believe this is a modern companies' basic requirement, which is to treat their employees like family members. Everyone is treated fairly. In return, they succeed in retaining talents from around the globe.

Failure in proper delegation

To get the most out of a situation, it is prudent that the work is divided suitably amongst the workforce. Leaders sometimes make a lapse in judgment when it comes to delegating duties, and it makes for ineffective leadership. Think about the friends you have when you are looking for advice. In order to get some real answers that would be helpful to you, you would not ask every one of your friends. You would take into consideration past experiences with those people and consider who is more adept with particular issues and who has been helpful before with this kind of issue.

Remember to use Neuro Linguistic Programming (NLP) to aid you in the delegation process. If you are unsure of your team members or employees' personality traits, ask them to take a test, which only takes a maximum of twenty minutes. Then, collect the data and analysis it.

For example, are you going to ask your friend who is mostly interested in art about how to design a webpage? Probably not, or you may get something fairly out of tune with what you were aiming for. Your friend who is a professional in art may not know how to code and build a proper and working website. You will have better results asking the friend involved in graphic or web design. Make sure that a person's skills are complementary to the tasks you are delegating to achieve the most favorable results. To get a better result, you can outsource it to someone else, such as a freelancer, website developer experts and website designer.

Those who are control freaks by nature will insist on doing most of the work themselves out of hesitation that nobody else would be able to do it properly - leading to unwarranted and extra stress. Leaders must learn how to delegate duties and not try to do everything by themselves because this is one of the most important tasks a good leader is capable of.

Insufficient feedback

It is vital for the team to be in the know-how about their merits and demerits on a particular project. Waiting for it to be the time for performance evaluations to let someone know of their mistake can prove fatal for the company. If there has been a mistake, then it is important to let your subordinate know right away so that they do not repeat it in the future.

If you do not address problems or mistakes when they are first presented they will inevitably lead into bigger ones. Think of it as the same as with your vehicle. If you ignore the strange sounds you have never heard before, it will cause the car to break down without the problem having been addressed and perhaps cause more serious work. Also, you will have missed the opportunity to address the issue while it is still fresh in the minds of everyone involved so that they can make a more conscious effort at correcting it. If you wait until a performance review to address something that happened months earlier, your employee will most likely take it less seriously or brush it off because the reality of the experience will have faded from their minds.

Does this mean that you must address every single issue when it presents itself, no matter how big or small? No, by then you will have wasted both yours and your employees' time getting caught up in the details. Focus on key points and explain them clearly, until your message is clearly understood. Weigh out the importance and relevance of what should be brought to your employees' attention by considering the bigger task at hand and the interim goals that will get you all there. Cushion the volume of long-term reviews by establishing regulated weekly, bi-weekly, or monthly performance assessments.

Feedback, whether good or bad, is as an important factor as any into the well functioning of a unit. Without feedback, it is like you lost of direction to head for. You have no idea about what have you done is right or wrong and what is working or not working.

Failure in providing rewards

Some leaders fail to acknowledge the time and effort put into achieving a goal by their employees. This in turn leads to a decrease in their self-esteem, questioning their value with the company. All work and no recognition eventually wears down on the psyche whether people are aware of it or not. Job tasks will appear to require more effort, workers become discouraged and lapses in productivity begin to occur. Resentment may set in. Some workers may feel underappreciated and if given long enough, will consider leaving the company for better prospects elsewhere. That would be a waste of all the training that particular member of staff has had during their employ in your company.

If workers are provided with incentives and rewards for their hard work, they will be further motivated to work better. They will work harder to achieve a bigger and higher incentives and rewards. When you receive a bonus from your company in commission or incentives or rewards, your day will be lightened up and motivation to work hard started to grow. You will want to consider exactly why you are rewarding an employee and make sure that it is aligned with the company's policies. Would you prefer them to get the job done faster while maintaining the integrity of quality? Would you want them to come in early and spend more time at work? Consider these objectives carefully and then construct a plan to highlight which behaviors are most valuable to your company. Customer care, improved leadership skills and averting apparent crises in high-risk businesses are all qualities to consider.

Then decide how you want to reward those behaviors. Many businesses miss out on the most cost-effective and morale-boosting incentives – recognition and appreciation. Showing recognition means making a public statement in front of coworkers and colleagues, commending a certain employee on a specific achievement they made. If done right, not only will it provide a boost in confidence for that employee, but it will provide incentive for the others to up their game as well. They will feel motivated for a period of time. Not only does the receiver of the compliment get motivated, but the other team members or employees also will become motivated and inspired to achieve similar goals for rewards shown. The other form is showing appreciation, which can be as simple as stopping by the employee's desk to congratulate them for their extra effort.

Orthodox outlook, resistance to change

A dead giveaway of a bad leader is his or her inability to change their ways. They are so set in their old ways, which they find comfortable, that they will stick to practicing those methods even when the future of the company is threatened. They do not realize the world is changing fast but they are still standing on same position, maybe for years or decades. Technology changes make us need to change too. Social media changes the way we communicate within the last ten years, especially Facebook, Whatsapp and Twitter. We tend to get information and news way faster and easier from the Internet than we ever could have in the past. By sitting in front your computer in your office, you can get to know what is happening in other countries. When bad leaders refuse to grow or change their management style or mindset, they will be left behind in a modern world. Respecting old practices is great, but not at the cost of the business. Even though you do not want to make changes, your competitors or partners will do it. If you fail to follow up and cannot get ahead of them, you will be left behind too. A fresh approach to things is sometimes the best option there is. Bad leaders restrict themselves while good leaders evolve. A good leader always gets new information and news that can influence their goals and applies them to learning. They are flexible to changes and welcome new ideas and knowledge. With new learning, they can apply it into their current challenges.

Ross Elkins

Chapter 10
The Future of Leadership

The world is evolving and won't stop for anything or anyone. This is what business leaders need to realize before thinking about their company's future.

If there are 2 challenges that almost every future leader will face and will eventually have to cope, then they can be classified as:

1. The pace of change,

2. The complexity with which challenges are surfacing,

3. Since the last decade, industries have been set to fast-forward and are changing rapidly. However, the recent recession in 2007 revealed that the pace couldn't be maintained forever and newer practices need to be introduced in order to keep the marketplace stable.

A particular set of interviews targeting CEOs showed that many of them were aware of the upcoming problems and grouped them as follows:

1. Volatile – the magnitude of the change cannot be predicted,

2. Uncertain – the precision & approximation with future could be predicted 50 years ago is no longer valid,

3. Complex – the difficulty level of tasks & assignments is always on the rise,

4. Ambiguous – leaders can easily get confused when figuring out the large-scale effects of their decisions,

Researchers have been working on these issues for quite some time now and have linked the increasing number of difficulties to a few elements. The first one of these is that workplaces nowadays contain too many interacting elements, right from secretaries to complex software. Secondly, information in the system can't be seen with clarity anymore and increased interaction makes the information even more confusing. Third, hindsight no longer leads to foresight as the environment is always dynamic.

The Skillset required for an efficient leader & manager have changed and the industry requires more complex thinkers than merely charismatic ones. Keeping all of the incoming & outgoing problems in mind, a leader must have the following skills:

- Adaptability,

- Boundary spanning,

- Self-awareness,

- Network thinking,

- Collaboration

It is now quite evident that the new environment is forcing leaders to change their traditional approach to a problem and turn to more dynamic ways. These dynamic techniques do not come on their own and require complex thinking capabilities. The leader must be open to skills & traits like agility, comfort, self-awareness, and strategic thinking. But the real question is, how will a leader produce or learn these skills?

Stakeholders worried about their CEOs and managers don't always need to bring a complete overhaul to their systems. They can start off small, simply by improving the quality of their leadership programs. It is increasingly being found that simply manufacturing leaders who can conjure creativity during crisis is not enough. Managers & executives are suggesting that the training programs are incomplete with respect to the pace with which the world has evolved and must be changed accordingly.

The most common ways of learning in training programs are as follows:

- Training,

- Job Assignments,

- Action learning,

- Executive coaching,

- Mentoring,

- 360 degree feedback

So what should be or can be done to solve this problem?

Methods that involve content-heavy training have become redundant & outdated and can no longer be relied on when training leaders for the future. Marshall Goldsmith spoke words of wisdom when she said that the world makes a fundamental mistake thinking that leaving something on its own will get it done one way or another.

There are a few trends that can be followed when training leaders; these can then greatly benefit both the individual as well as the organization.

Trend 1: Greater Focus on Vertical Development

What do you think should be removed or altered from the current way of leadership development to make it more effective? The question was asked from a group of executives, and the following replies were received in abundance:

- Competencies – they can become overwhelming and add to stress if not managed properly. If the company is starting out then they might not be that hard to handle, but with the passage of time ditching them would be the right thing to do.

- Competencies – they don't add value to the firm,

- Competency models – they are outdated and no longer valid,

- Competencies – still okay for new executives but can't be used for training senior executives,

It can be seen that most CEOs regard competency models as an outdated concept which is best when applied to fresh intakes.

Why did the world discard these models all of a sudden? The reason executives started to rule-out competency models was because they failed to point out fundamental differences between the 2 core types of development, namely vertical & horizontal.

Horizontal development is referred to as the development of new skills, approaches and abilities. It can be thought of as technical learning. The technique comes in most handy when a problem is defined and the method for solving it exists & has precedent. A well-established example of horizontal development is surgery training. Students learn the technique by going through a vetted process known as pimping in which professional surgeons question students until they can no longer answer the question, forcing them to go back and learn. The process may not be the easiest one but nonetheless it gets the job done and every time the student is forced to come back with something new.

On the other hand, vertical development is more concerned about the stages required to get a job/task done. The best example of vertical development is that of children who progress through a number of stages as they grow however common sense assumes that this process comes to a halt as soon as they hit the age of 20. However, further research into the topic has revealed that human beings keep on growing "mentally" even after the age of 20 at varying yet predictable rates. At each stage, the adult becomes more aware of the world and understands more complex situations as compared to when he/she was younger.

In metaphorical terms, horizontal development can be analogized as pouring water into a glass. The glass fills up in the same way you learn new leadership techniques. But vertical development focusses on expanding the glass altogether as it fills up, thus making it able to retain greater volume or more leadership capabilities in retrospect. Not only does the glass increase its capacity but the structure changes as well, forcing the individual to become more intelligent and develop a degree of greater complexity. From a technological standpoint, adding a new software to a computer can be thought of as horizontal development while upgrading the computer altogether is known as vertical development. A lot of people are quite aware of the fact that adding new software to an old computer will make it slower, thus vertical development is preferred over horizontal development.

Horizontal development along with competency models however can't totally be ruled out as they will remain an important part when developing company leadership. One of the interviewees during the leadership session stated that its time for the world to both transcend & include the competency mentality so that companies can grow their leaders in both horizontal & vertical directions. John McGuire & Gary Rhodes of Center for Creative Leadership say that organizations have focused and successfully grown skilled at the development of competencies but have ignored transforming their leader's mind from one level to the next so that it can absorb more information.

Today's marketplace requires a leader to grow vertically if he is to stay at the top of his game, otherwise he would end up delegating most of his powers when he would be unable to process more information, that would lead to diminishing his vision to some extent.

Why does vertical development matter when it comes to leadership?

Many of you might still be wondering the exact reasons as to why vertical development is required when grooming a leader. From a leadership standpoint, researchers have repeatedly shown that people that have a higher level of development give better performances in difficult environments. Keith Eigel carried out an ambitious study targeting 21 CEOs and 21 managers from different companies each with a revenue of 5 Billion USD per year. The study came up with the conclusion that across a range of leadership measures, there was a sharp relation between vertical development and effectiveness. The findings have then been replicated on a number of other studies, confirming their conclusion.

When it comes to managers, the basic reason as to why they're able to perform with greater effectiveness is because they can think in a multi-dimensional manner. McGuire & Rhodes also came to the conclusion that each successive level of leadership holds not only greater knowledge but also greater capacity for learning. The leader is able to set new direction for the company and lead people with greater emotion. In addition, vertical development also helps people improve their adaptation rate which means that they can come up with efficient strategies in a shorter time period.

Inherently speaking, there is nothing better about being at a higher level of development. Being an adolescent doesn't mean you're "better" than a toddler. But looking at the facts you find that an adolescent is able to handle situations of greater complexity compared to a toddler. Any level of development can fit a situation; the main question is that can the level of development solve the problem or issue at hand?

In terms of leadership, if you think that the future environments will be complex, unpredictable and volatile then you must also understand that organizations that focus on vertical development will have a better chance of handling and adapting to those environments.

What do the stages of development look like?

There are a number of frameworks that are used by researchers to measure & describe various levels of cognitive development. The 3 stages of Keagan's Adult Levels of Development are as follows:

- 3-socialized mind: at this stage our mind is shaped by the opinions & expectations of those surrounding us.

- 4-self-authoring mind: we have developed a consistent ideology of our own and an internal navigation system. The mind has successfully developed its belief system, values and conducts. Any leader can take stand for himself and set limits on his own.

- 5-Self-transforming mind: we have an ideology of our own but now see it as limited. The mind is able to make decisions based on knowledge and not on a single perspective.

The following table will help you understand the levels of development:

Level	Kegan Levels	CCL Action Logics	Torbert & Rookes Logic
5	Self-transforming	Interdependent-collaborator	Ironist (>1%), Alchemist (2%), Strategist (5%)
4	Self-authoring	Independent-achiever	Individualist (11%), Achiever (30%), Expert (37%)
3	Socialized	Dependent-conformer	Diplomat (11%), Opportunist (4%)

What causes Vertical Development?

The techniques required for horizontal development are quite different from vertical development, the main one being that the former can be learnt from an expert whereas the latter requires learning from one's own self. Researchers have been carrying out researches on the topic for the past 75 years and have come to the following conclusion:

- People feel frustrated when they're constantly faced with situations, challenges or dilemmas,

- The challenge or situation forces them to feel the limit of their current manner of thinking,

- It is an area of their life about which they deeply care about,

- There is adequate amount of support that enables people to stand in the face of conflict,

Development movement from one stage to the next is heavily driven by limitations in the current level. When a person is confronted with a number of challenges that require an altered manner of thinking, he/she has no other option but to take the next step. This accelerates development and within a short period of time the person is able to handle tasks of similar complexity quite easily.

Vertical development is a three-fold process:

1. Awaken - the individual becomes aware of the existence of other methodologies & techniques to solve a problem,

2. Unlearn & discern – the assumptions held in the past are first analyzed and then rejected accordingly. New assumptions are rolled in and tested out.

3. Advance – occurs after some effort & practice and requires a person to have a strong mindset to dominate the previous ideas.

In addition, it has also been found that cognitive development cannot only be limited to individual level but can also be raised to an organizational level. If an organization wishes to be successful in the long term then raising leaders alone won't be enough; it should also work to develop a leadership culture in the workplace. The process starts from the top and ends up at the bottom.

Trend 2: Transfer of Greater Developmental Ownership to the Individual

A number of people were asked the following question:

What should be phased out in the process of leadership development?

Almost everyone replied with, "Stop forcing people to study courses they don't have interest in".

The rule not only applies in a professional environment but in an academic one as well in which many students are forced to take courses according to their parents' demands. Social psychologists have repeatedly shown that people's motivation is at the highest level when they feel as if they have some power over their decisions. However, for the past 50 years or so, organizations have bred dependency in people to such an extent that they feel like they're mere passengers in the development journey. A number of managers still see themselves as being monitored and owned by someone else rather than their own selves.

The culture has bred to such a level that even after the introduction of methods like performance feedback, mentoring and action learning, CEOs and managers still think it's someone else' job to tell them what to do or how to be better at something. The best example of such behavior is outsourcing work to other companies who might know how to do something but don't hold the same level of passion as you do. The main challenge faced when solving this problem is bringing people back into the driver seat so that they could take charge of their own development.

Many researchers think that the issue mentioned previously has been solved to quite an extent in the past 10 years as the demand of leaders to take on managerial roles increased. Despite workers' doubts about the current approach to development methods, there are a number of signs that show that in the future there will be a growing demand for executive level coaching.

Here are some modifying factors for coaching:

- The manager/CEO holds the power to choose the direction,

- The process will be customized for every person,

- The coach is simply there for guidance, not leading,

- The coach must be seen as a partner and not an expert,

- The process will take time and not take shape instantly,

Coaching may be in demand but for many organizations the process is too costly and time taking. Instead, if organizations could transfer the coaching process back to their own staff, they could save a ton of money and be better in touch with the workings of the organization. Furthermore, the leadership wouldn't have to worry about losing trade secrets.

An example that increases ownership:

What is it?

A behavior change process that is designed for busy individuals looking for measurable results. In the feedforward process and individual kicks off a coaching process along with trusted, fellow colleagues. Each of the colleagues is asked to do 3 things:

- Focus on the future,

- Give only suggestions,

- Make these something positive the person can do,

How it works?

Participants will choose 1 – 2 areas which they want to improve and engage 5 – 8 trusted colleagues who will act as feedforward coaches. With the support of these coaches, the person gathers suggestions about the field he/she needs to improve. After 6 – 8 months, the findings are gathered and level of behavioral change throughout the time period is analyzed.

Why it works?

The process is efficient and takes only 2 – 3 hours/month. It involves only the people a person trust so is safe. This also ensures that accurate suggestions about the person are given as the people are usually quite close. In addition, by accepting others as his coach, the person acknowledges the process. Feedforward coaching puts the leader under development in the driving seat and lets him/her make the decisions. For instance, the person will collect suggestions from his coaches and then think of best ways to implement them. This gives the person maximum power.

Trend 3 – Decline of Heroism & Rise of Collective Leadership

During the last 50 years leadership development was more focused on certain individuals in an organization rather than the workplace as a whole. The leader came up with ways in which the organization can make more profit or can become efficient and after implementing the ideas successfully was called an excellent leader. However, in the last 15 years this particular model is losing its charm as the "fit" between difficulties of the workplace and the ability of a single person to solve them in a "heroic" manner has widened. The complexity of the new environment has brought forward a number of challenges that are impossible for one person to solve. Instead, these complex problems require a collective effort often consisting of executives from different fields.

A simple solution for these problems is teaching managers the techniques that could bring together various executives. As executives alone cannot collaborate, share and discuss, they need a binding entity which can be delegated to a high level manager. Many researchers have stated that this is the end of an era for individual leadership and beginning for networks of leadership. The field of innovation has kick-started this process. Previously, it was thought by almost all employees that innovation came from "eureka" moments, but now it is being found that innovations are more dependent on the type of collective effort put by many rather than one man.

In a similar manner, leadership has long been held up by heroic personalities who always seem to save the day in command & inspire style organizations. The idea resonated with the public for quite some time who started following successful individual leaders to become like them. But as the problems became more complex, even those individual leaders required a lot of "technical consultants" and problem solving became a multi-faced process not a lone, decisive one.

The transition in thinking won't come easy or quickly. For instance, the entire world looked for the leader who was behind toppling the leadership of Hosni Mubarak, the Egyptian President but couldn't find one as the leadership consisted of open ended youth networks directing the movement from social networks. It was quite clear that the movement had a "we" factor to it rather than an "a' factor. The younger generation's comfort & fluidity with social networks mean they can work better when they're connected with each other and provide suggestions that can move an organization forward.

Redefining Leadership:

The process of shifting towards collective leadership can be started by changing the definition of the word "leadership" and implementing it within an organization. The trend of shifting from individual leadership to multi-level leadership has been increasing. The process, for instance may be defined as:

- The process of arranging & using people to face difficulties,

- Anyone who gets in place and helps the organization come closer to its goals,

- Leaders are people in an organization who are involved in the processes of producing, direction, alignment and commitment.

The major theme of what the 3rd trend states is that a leader can be anyone and the position is no longer tied to a stage/level in a hierarchy. In fact, some researchers think that it is much easier to exercise powers from a position outside authority than within an authority and all the constraints that come with it.

Leadership becomes free to be distributed throughout vast networks that are irrespective of boundaries both geographical and mental. In such an organization, the question, who is the leader becomes much less important than what is needed in the system & how it will be done.

If leadership is thought of as a shared process then the organization is more likely to flourish as collectively set of executives will have more insight over an issue. This will result in:

- Open flow of information,

- Flexible hierarchies,

- Distributed resources,

- Easier decision making,

- Lesser centralized control,

Organizations that embrace the above mentioned conditions and align themselves with the sweeping, new range of technologies are more likely to have an upper hand when the change becomes mandatory. The most common example of such a revolution in technological terms is as follows:

1. Web 1.0 (1999 – 2000) – this involved tools for easier communication becoming widespread and being used in almost every company in the world.

2. Web 2.0 (2001 – 2010) – this introduced a set of upgraded tools and methodologies for communication & interaction.

3. Web 3.0 (2011 – present) – more powerful and revolutionary platforms like cloud computing were introduced and meta-level methods for managing knowledge pools become widespread.

While the world is still in the early stages of thinking about leadership development at a collective level, the world nonetheless needs to carry out research on the area so that future generations won't be tied up at the hierarchical level in the same old-fashioned way. With socialization tools on the rise, hierarchies need to become flat and control needs to be decentralized.

Conclusion

Thank you for choosing this book. I hope it has been a satisfying read for you.

Leadership is a necessary trait for any high-ranking position in any organization. While some possess a natural leadership attitude, in others, it has to be manifested through careful practice and guidance. You need to experience a lot of failures and stand up taller to become stronger. Rome was not built in a day. This book aimed to help you to do just that. Leaders cannot be made overnight, but this book aims at providing you with pointers, tips and insight into becoming a better leader so you can perform well in the workspace. My aim is to guide and give you better understanding so you will become a successful leader as well.

Effective leadership is all about providing a vision and motivating your team members to work towards achieving the same goal.

Ross Elkins

There are a wide variety of qualities that make a good leader, as discussed in the book previously. In the book, also outlined, are the things expected from a good leader, strategies for leading in business, pointers on how to coach your subordinates, and what not to do in order to be a good leader.

Acting in a leadership position does not mean that you are set in a role and cannot evolve. Leadership is about doing new things and playing with the possible outcomes till you get satisfactory results. Put the insight offered in this book to good use and improve your leadership skills to get optimum results in the workplace.

I hope you have found the book helpful, and will continue to refer to it in the future to help build yourself a successful leadership profile. I hope it was able to teach you the skills of an effective leader and the necessary outlook that one must have in order to succeed in the world of the corporate lifestyle.

I also hope you take the time to study this book, and I hope that climbing the corporate ladder becomes easier for you because of the knowledge that you have gained here. Your new skills, mindset, your knowledge and hard work are all you need to make it in the corporate world and surpass your current supervisors without hesitation.

If you have ever wanted to be your boss's boss, this book will get you there without much struggle. Give it time and all you've got. Soon, you will be more than you ever dreamed of. Showing leadership skills will get you there.

Good luck on your endeavors in the corporate world! I wish you success, happiness and a lot of promotions.

Complete Your Business Relationship Skills Education with a Click Away

Management: Golden Nugget Methods to Manage Effectively - Teams, Personnel Management, Management Skills, and Conflict Resolution

Communication: Golden Nugget Methods to Communicate Effectively - Interpersonal, Influence, Social Skills, Listening

Take Your Business Skills Further for Financial Freedom or Corporate Dominance:

Small Business: EXACT BLUEPRINT on How to Start a Business - Home Business, Entrepreneur, and Small Business Marketing

Marketing: Golden Nuggets to Market Effectively - Internet Marketing, E-Commerce, Advertising & Web Marketing

Sales: Foolproof Method to CRUSH Your Numbers - Selling, Sales Techniques, and Sales Strategy

Ross Elkins

13128749R00142

Printed in Great Britain
by Amazon.co.uk, Ltd.,
Marston Gate.